DEAD MEN RULING

DEAD MEN RULING

How to Restore Fiscal Freedom
and Rescue Our Future

C. Eugene Steuerle

A PROJECT OF THE URBAN INSTITUTE
AND THE CENTURY FOUNDATION

The Century Foundation Press • New York

Library of Congress cataloging-in-publication data available on request from the publisher.

Manufactured in the United States of America

Cover design by Abby Grimshaw
Text design by Cynthia Stock

This book is dedicated to my wife, Marge,
my children, step children and grandchildren—
all of whom are forced to listen to me when
the rest of you can simply put down the book.

Contents

Preface

Low or zero growth in employment . . . inadequate funds to pay future Social Security and Medicare bills . . . declining rates of investment . . . cuts in funding for education and children's programs . . . arbitrary sequesters or cutbacks in good and bad programs alike . . . underfunded pension plans . . . bankrupt cities . . . threats not to pay our nation's debts . . . inability to reach political compromise . . . political parties with no real vision for twenty-first-century government.

I have come to a strong belief that these and a whole host of seemingly separable economic and political problems are symptoms of a common disease, one unique to our time and shared widely throughout the developed world. Unless that disease and the history of how it spread over time is understood, it is easy to fall prey to believing in simple but ineffective nostrums, hoping that a cure lies merely in switching political parties or reducing the deficit, expanding our favorite program, or hunkering down to protect it. My first purpose in writing this book is to accurately diagnose that disease so we can attack it at its roots

But my fonder hope is that we reawaken to the extraordinary possibilities that lay right at our feet and restore the American can-do spirit that has prevailed over most of our history. Despite the despairing claims of many, we no more live in an age of austerity than did Americans at the turn into the twentieth century with the demise of the frontier. Conditions are ripe to advance opportunity in ways never before possible, including doing for children and the young in this century what the twentieth did for senior citizens, yet without abandoning those earlier gains. Recognizing this extraordinary but checked potential is also the secret to breaking the political logjam that, as I will show, was created largely by now dead (and retired) men.

Acknowledgments

It is impossible to convey my very deep indebtedness to so many people. First of all to Larry Haas, you have been an incredible collaborator and colleague in helping me write and edit this book. You know, and I know, that you deserve a lot more credit than I can ever give to you. To my research assistants, Caleb Quakenbush, Katherine Toran, and Ellen Steele, you have been patient, thorough, and amazingly talented in editing, finding sources, graphing, and in so many other ways helping me through the many months of this project. I am especially grateful for a Presidential Discretionary Grant from the Foundation for Child Development, a sign of belief in me that was also crucial to completing this work. To Janice Nittoli, president, and Jason Renker, editorial director, at The Century Foundation, thanks so much pulling it all together, editing it into final publication form, and, most of all, believing in me.

1 | Introduction: The Challenge at Hand

As for the future, your task is not to foresee it, but to enable it.

—Antoine de Saint-Exupéry

The United States has always been a nation of groundbreaking achievement, spurred by a sense of mission and destiny. It has been that way from even before its official founding, from the time that Governor John Winthrop told his shipmates aboard the *Arbella* in 1630, "For we must consider that we shall be as a city upon a hill. The eyes of all people are upon us."[1]

Over the next nearly four centuries, this new breed of people created the modern world's first functioning democracy; carved a bustling coast-to-coast country out of a wilderness of forests, mountains, and rivers; led allied nations to victory in two world wars; expanded civil rights and opportunity across the far reaches of society; explored the moon; won the Cold War; and developed the richest, most powerful nation known to history.

Fast forward to today, a time of economic uncertainty and political disarray. A profound change has dampened the nation's aspirations, reflecting a pervasive pessimism that stalks the land and replaces the "can-do" spirit that has dominated our history. On challenge after challenge—from educating our children to rebuilding our highways, from reforming our government to investing more in our future—the nation is enduring a bout of tentativeness and uncertainty.

Policymakers blame this "can't-do" resignation on our large past and projected future budget deficits. We can't do things, they say, because

1

we do not have the money. Yes, a cash-strapped government will be hard-pressed to find the money to fund new priorities. Yes, policymakers must eventually reduce the deficits that are expected to mount in the coming years for all sorts of compelling reasons—from finding ourselves without the resources to meet the next economic crisis, to reducing our borrowing from unfriendly foreign countries, to preventing our long-term economic decline.

But those who focus solely on surging deficits miss the forest for the trees. Deficits are but a symptom of a much broader disease: *the effort by both political parties to control the future.* In trying to impose their agendas on the future, they deprive today's generation and those to come of the right to determine their own futures.

My thesis is quite simple. In recent decades, both parties have conspired to create and expand a series of public programs that automatically grow so fast that they claim every dollar of additional tax revenue that the government generates each year. They also have conspired to lock in tax cuts that leave the government unable to pay its bills. The resulting squeeze deprives current and future generations of the leeway to choose their own priorities, allocate their own resources, and reach for their own stars. Those generations are left largely to maintain yesterday's priorities.

Unlike reaching the moon, rejuvenating the economy, winning a war, or curing a disease, none of these permanent programs are designed to achieve goals or solve problems once and for all. Almost all of them simply maintain, and often perpetually increase, subsidies for some pattern of consumption—overpriced health care, more years in retirement, or bigger McMansions. Meanwhile, even in good economic times, we refuse to pay our bills. We are left with a budget for a declining nation that invests ever-less in our future, particularly in our children, and a broken government that presides over archaic, inefficient, and inequitable spending and tax programs.

We can fix this problem, but we must see it clearly. We must discard the notion that we are just short of cash, that our budgets are merely unbalanced. We must remove the straightjacket on us, our children, and children to come. Only then can today's and future generations shape their own destinies.

The forces of history have put us at a major turning point, one requiring that we restore flexibility to voters and their government. We cannot do so without a fundamental reform or big fix in which both political parties remove the shackles they have placed on the public and themselves. And while deficit reduction agreements or even grand bargains, aimed at preventing debt from exploding might be necessary, they ultimately would address only a symptom of a wider disease and, hence, will ultimately disappoint us.

What is required is nothing less than a drive to free up resources so we can again make the types of choices that Americans made for over two centuries about how government should evolve. In practical terms, Democrats must agree to limit the automatic growth that policymakers typically build into major health, retirement, and other key spending programs; and Republicans must agree to do likewise for tax subsidies so that over time we can generate the revenues needed to pay current bills rather than pass on more debt to future generations.

A big fix like this would allow future voters to focus on the problems and opportunities of their own time, allowing them to better decide the size and nature of any governmental response that they want to pursue. With such budgetary freedom restored, I believe that the nation would then turn its attention to today's needs, namely an agenda of investment (particularly for children), opportunity, mobility, efficiency and fairness—an agenda that still allows for lean government because policymakers would design programs for success and continual reassessment, not for eternal built-in growth.

By shifting the budget toward investment in education, early childhood development, and other priorities set by evidence of high potential impact, we would promote growth for both the nation and its people over the long term. Think of the twenty-first century as doing for the young what the twentieth did for the elderly, only with a focus this time on opportunity and potential, not simply a higher level of consumption throughout our lives.

By reducing tax and other disincentives to work and saving, we would create more opportunity for families at all levels to move up the economic ladder.

By keeping our government lean, we would rediscover that we have the ability to shift resources to new priorities.

I imagine a reinvigorated government with the flexibility and vigor to enact a forward-looking agenda of this kind—a government that can respond to new needs, adapt to new economic forces, and seize new prospects. I envision a government that enables the generations of today and tomorrow to shape their own destiny and make the choices that are rightfully theirs.

To create this future, we must first restore *fiscal freedom*.

To Govern Is To Choose

For most of American history—from the founding of the republic to at least the end of World War II—the reality of governing in Washington reflected the truism, "To govern is to choose." Each year, our elected leaders decided which programs to fund and how to finance them. They set new priorities based on the challenges at hand, be they war or recession, poverty or hunger, civil strife or economic injustice.

Despite rancorous debates, our leaders normally had much more fiscal freedom—the leeway to set priorities, shift direction, and respond to new challenges—than they do today. That was true during both liberal times when government's share of the economy grew, and conservative times when it shrank.

Why? Because the president and Congress created and funded programs mostly on a year-to-year basis, extending them only after first considering other ways to use available revenues.

Meanwhile, as the economy expanded, revenues grew from year to year. Every quarter-century or so, annual revenues tended to double, whether generated by a tariff or an income tax. For a president elected for two terms, revenues would typically grow by roughly one-third during his tenure—even when Congress did not formally raise taxes. So, even when the nation's leaders extended programs that were already in place, economic growth generated new revenues with which to confront new challenges.

In fact, due to these rising revenues, almost any budget that the president and Congress enacted in any year would have translated into massive budget surpluses in future years, if policymakers had merely kept those same laws in place. Deficits might arise at some points in time if, for instance, policymakers cut taxes to revive the economy or greatly boosted military spending to win a war. But those deficits, if they occurred, were driven by the legislation of the day, not by decisions made in the past.

In recent decades, however, the policymaking process in Washington has changed profoundly. Increasingly tempted by the desire to create eternal legacies, both parties have sought to create and fund spending programs not just each year, but on a permanent basis, or to set taxes below the levels required to fund the government shaped by those permanent programs.

If each piece of legislation is looked at in isolation, the motives of both parties seem laudatory, their goals reasonable. They wanted to provide a measure of economic certainty on which current and future Americans could rely for the entirety of their lives. After all, families across America have to plan for the long term. They must assess how much they will need for their children's education, what's required to live comfortably in retirement, and what rewards they will get for working, saving, and investing. Businesses want to know how much their profits will be taxed. The more long-term economic security and planning certainty that government can help provide to families and businesses, the better.

Liberals focus on issues such as poverty and inequality, on the problems of middle- and low-income Americans in making ends meet, feeding their families, finding decent places to live, securing health care for themselves and their children, and saving for retirement. Naturally, they stress efforts to provide retirement security for senior citizens; to provide health insurance for the aged, the poor, and the uninsured; to expand access to higher education; to eliminate hunger; and to help the unemployed and the poor.

Conservatives focus on issues such as freedom and the size of government, on whether government will restrict opportunity or discourage work, saving, and growth by taxing families and regulating businesses. Naturally, they have been more associated with efforts to cut taxes and keep them low.

The problem arises when the balance between fiscal freedom, on the one hand, and guarantees of future certainty, on the other, tilts too much toward the latter. That is where we—and, indeed, much of the developed world—are today, and where we will increasingly be in the future. That is also where we will remain if we think that merely reducing deficits will solve our problems.

On the spending side, the budget for the past several decades has become increasingly dominated by programs—informally known as "entitlements"—particularly those that grow automatically.[2] The biggest, most popular, and fastest growing center on retirement and health, including the "Big Three": Social Security, Medicare, and Medicaid. These entitlements and some related tax subsidies provide benefits and services to Americans based on age, income, or other criteria, and they remain in place and grow from year to year, unless the president and Congress enact laws to change them.

Most of these health and retirement programs automatically grow very fast, because policymakers designed them to do so. No matter what new needs or priorities arise, these programs require ever-higher federal spending (as shares of both the budget and our economy) as people live longer, benefits grow along with wages, new health goods and services become available, and health prices rise. Over and above this automatic growth, policymakers also have expanded eligibility for these programs, as well as the benefits and services they provide, which boosts the budgets of these programs even more. Then, when recession or a declining growth in the labor force (due to falling birth rates) moves the budget from balance to deficit, these programs nonetheless keep growing.

The more such entitlements grow—and the greater the share of federal spending that they assume—the more such automatic spending reduces the fiscal freedom of voters and the officials they elect.

That certain health and retirement programs grow automatically over time may sound reasonable, with the population aging and health care costs rising. But they were growing very fast even before the population was aging as it is today, and they are a major cause of, not just a response to, rising health costs. Consider: we do not automatically increase our funding for defense or education forever into the future, even when we view a strong military and a good education system as national priorities. Instead, we make non-entitlement programs, which include most basic functions of government, compete for federal dollars on a yearly or at least periodic basis.

On the tax side, policymakers have cut top personal income tax rates from 91 percent—the level before President Kennedy's individual tax cut (enacted a few months after his death)—to between 28 percent and 40 percent in the years since 1986. At the same time, they have carved more credits and deductions into the tax code, including new health credits and tax breaks for contributions to 401(k) plans, while allowing other subsidies, such as the home mortgage interest deduction, to continue expanding from year to year—with much of the additional costs simply subsidizing those who have the most money to begin with.

Moreover, policymakers have limited federal tax burdens to an average of about 18 percent of gross domestic product (GDP) in recent decades, and lower still as the twenty-first century dawned—even though spending has risen to an average of more than 21 percent of GDP a year and is scheduled (through these automatically rising obligations) to approach 25 percent or more.[3] The more that elected officials cut taxes and thereby boost budget deficits, and the more that they block tax hikes designed simply to pay current bills, the more they shift burdens to future generations in the form of higher debt and interest payments on that debt. The more they deny government a key tool—higher taxes—to finance new priorities, the more they, too, shrink fiscal freedom.

To show the unique nature of our current problem and why deficit cutting in some traditional sense will not solve it, my colleague Tim Roeper and I developed a "fiscal democracy index" (see Figure 1.1) to document the fall in the fiscal freedom of policymakers in recent years and into the future.

This index measures the extent to which past and future projected revenues are already claimed by the permanent programs that are now in place (including interest payments on the debt). The fiscal democracy index is neutral; it favors neither a liberal or conservative agenda in

Figure 1.1. *Steuerle-Roeper Fiscal Democracy Index*

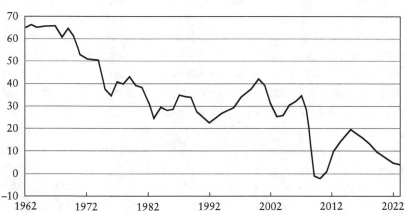

Source: Author's calculations from OMB Historical Tables and CBO February 2013 Budget and Economic Outlook.

that it falls with both rising spending mandated from the past as well as reduced revenues.

Much more is at stake than just reduced budget flexibility when fiscal freedom is dramatically curtailed. Democracy itself begins to creak and function poorly when previous decisions by dead and retired policymakers effectively curtail today's and future generations of the power to make their own decisions. The lower the index, the less freedom that current voters and elected officials can exercise their traditional democratic rights to vote on the future direction of government unless—and this is a big "unless"—they first obtain a type of supermajority (for example, majority support by both houses of Congress and the president) to overturn or renege on past promises built into the law.

The potential effects on democracy are apparent to all who open their eyes: the crazy U.S. patterns of sequesters, government shut-downs, partisanship, inability to legislate, along with Tea Party and Occupy Wall Street protests with little real forward-looking agendas, combine with increasingly archaic programs focused on the past, not the future. Though our focus here is on the American story, the even greater lack of fiscal freedom in many parts of Western Europe has often led to even more dysfunctional government and more violent protests to a changing order that simply can no longer stand.

The U.S. index fell into negative territory for the first time ever in 2009—meaning that every dollar of revenue had been committed before the new Congress walked through the Capitol doors. Revenues for the first time in U.S. history fell short of the built-in spending of permanent programs—and it will return to negative territory as soon as a decade from now if the president and Congress do not change current entitlement and tax policies. Even efforts, such as those scheduled in much of current law, to reduce annual non-entitlement spending toward zero— thus, ending most education, transportation, housing, defense, and most other general government programs—will do little to alter the downward path of the index other than reduce interest costs temporarily. That means that future generations will have no additional revenues to finance their own new priorities, and they will have to raise taxes or cut other spending just to finance the expected growth in existing programs.

Nothing that either party is considering these days will prevent the situation from simply getting worse. With many entitlement programs growing automatically, the baby boomers starting to retire in ever-increasing numbers, and federal revenues falling further behind, all future revenues will again be committed (actually, overcommitted) to meet the promises that previous presidents and Congresses have made. Which constitutional framer would have thought that, by the turn of the twenty-first century, lawmakers had already attempted to determine the budget for 2030, 2070, 2100, and even beyond?

In essence, dead and retired policymakers put America on a budget path in which spending will grow faster than any conceivable growth in revenues—even if the president and Congress never create any other spending program. The same policymakers also cut taxes so much below spending that they created huge deficits, which have now compounded the problem with additional debt and the corresponding requirement to make higher interest payments to government bondholders.

To be sure, what yesterday's lawmakers have done, today's can undo. The fast-growing spending programs and low taxes are not set in stone, imposed from the heavens. But they are set in law and, in the real world of policymaking, changing the law to break past promises to voters is easier said than done.

Watch any race for president or Congress. Each candidate talks about all the wonderful new benefits and tax cuts he or she will enact on our behalf, while talking only vaguely about who will face counterbalancing higher taxes or lower benefits (typically, the target for such pain is some small group like millionaires or welfare recipients, never the broad middle class). Each also attacks any opponent who tries to talk honestly about the cost of government and about imposing substantial spending cuts or tax increases to pay for future obligations.

Generous benefits and low taxes create public expectations, and Americans have come to rely on a government that only collects $60 to $90 for every $100 it spends. The "entitlement" expectation stretches ever upward to all income classes. Many of the rich now expect to pay lower tax rates than the not-so-rich, the middle class to retire in late middle age and let someone else pay the bill, and the poor to avoid any quid-pro-quo for the benefits they receive. That political reality creates real obstacles to well-meaning efforts to change course, re-shape our built-in spending and tax regimes, and reverse the decline in fiscal freedom.

In essence, we suffer from a disease that is unique in modern history: both parties have competed to control all—or more than all—of the revenues that will likely flow to policymakers of the future, not just the present. Because programs already in place will claim those revenues, yesterday's policymakers have robbed their successors of their fiscal freedom.

Serving the Past, Failing the Future

Our government is increasingly frozen in time, with both the spending and tax sides assuming the mantle of permanence. The more permanent the budget, the greater the share of spending determined by previous decisions, the less fiscal freedom that today's policymakers have to shift dollars to new priorities, respond to new problems, and seize new opportunities.

Both sides have largely achieved their central policy goals—liberals have expanded social welfare programs, conservatives have delivered lower taxes. Both now cling tenaciously to their victories. Neither will seriously consider visions of a future government that do not reflect any aspect of those victories. Liberals will not rethink social welfare programs, even for elderly couples who are soon scheduled to receive an average of more than $1 million in old age benefits; conservatives will not abandon their push for ever-lower lower tax rates, regardless of whether the top income tax rates at the time are 90 percent or 40 percent. That working together they might better address the problems that bedevil America with a different approach seems not to faze them. To the ramparts they go—for the status quo.

As older generations of liberals and conservatives fight to retain their policy victories, younger Americans increasingly feel ignored by the political process. They often tune out the policy debate altogether, gathering more information from the late-night satires of Jon Stewart and Stephen Colbert than from policy advocates fighting to retain their past victories.

Unfortunately, a permanent budget is, by definition, a budget that is increasingly out of date for the nation it purports to serve. The budget may move in directions set by previous policymakers, with the health and retirement entitlements dominating spending and low tax burdens dominating revenues and adding to interest costs. But neither the economy nor the society move the same way.

The nation's leaders created the income tax in 1913, Social Security in 1935, and Medicare and Medicaid in 1965. While those programs increasingly dominate the fiscal picture, the decades since their creation have brought breath-taking change to the United States as well as to America's place in the world.

We are much richer and more powerful; our people are much more racially and ethnically diverse, and they live longer and have fewer children to support them in old age; our economy is far less dependent on agriculture and manufacturing and far more dominated by the service, high-tech, and information sectors; our businesses face more competition from abroad; the jobs of the future will increasingly demand more education and skills than those of yesterday; our universities remain the envy of the world, but we are saddling the young with more and more debt to attend them; we are falling behind on such social indicators as educational test scores and infant mortality; and we are falling behind as well on technologies for which the government must lead, whether in areas such as space technology or in integrated health information systems to fight disease.

With the world, the nation, the economy, and society changing at an ever-swifter pace, we have a budget not for a nation that is preparing for its future but rather one that is nostalgic for its past, a budget not for an ever-rising nation but for a declining one. Rather than think anew, liberals want only to protect and expand the same social welfare structure that they began building more than a half-century ago. Rather than think anew, conservatives want only to ensure that Congress does not raise tax burdens, cut back on tax breaks, raise the top marginal income tax rate, or even tax capital gains at all. Together, they are like lawmakers who, after the Civil War had settled the issue of slavery, still wanted to debate the Missouri Compromise of 1820.

In both the United States and many European nations, which are facing similar crises, policymakers recently have been tempted to believe that they can solve their nation's ills by treating a symptom—deficits. As much as that may be necessary, it is not sufficient. The problem will remain even if policymakers find a way to reduce surging deficits or temporarily balance the budget.

History proves it. The United States has faced growing federal deficits before—as recently as the 1980s and early 1990s. In response, presidents and members of Congress from both parties enacted five major deficit-reduction agreements from 1982 to 1997, most of them a combination of spending cuts and tax increases, and they managed to balance the budget for four straight years from 1998 through 2001. But, if their achievement reduced the risks of a deficit-driven economic crisis and brought other economic benefits, it did little to reverse the trend of declining fiscal freedom. The budget was briefly in balance, but the long-term budget problem remained. Retirement and health entitlements kept growing, tax burdens fell, and policymakers continued to see their fiscal freedom slip away.[4]

History, alas, also repeats itself. Large deficits reappeared in the first decade of the twenty-first century and ballooned during the Great Recession of 2007 to 2009 and the years that followed. Elected officials soon came to realize that something was amiss, but they, too, continue to focus on the symptom of short-run deficits, not the longer-term causes of reduced fiscal freedom. They mainly focus on programs that have little connection to the causes of our disease—the non-entitlement spending that they set year to year and that funds the day-to-day operations of government (for example, defense, homeland security, education, research, science, space, food safety, and law enforcement)—while, at best, they fiddle with entitlements and adequate revenues at the margins. They change budget policy for a few years at most while avoiding the promises in place that, if not addressed, will ensure shrinking fiscal freedom for generations to come.

As policymakers reduce short-term deficits, that will not be enough to restore fiscal freedom—just as the era of deficit cutting two decades ago did little to create possibilities for the future. Health, retirement, and other growing entitlements will continue to absorb an ever-larger share of spending, and tax burdens will prove increasingly inadequate to fund the government at hand. Unless policymakers confront, head-on, what it means to restore fiscal freedom, future generations will have no opportunity to set the priorities and fund the programs they want.

That is why the problem is not the deficit; that is a symptom, not the disease.

Now, let us imagine a different world.

Let us imagine that we aspire to continue building a "city upon a hill," rather than merely fight over who is entitled to rewards from the sacrifices of past builders. Let us imagine a world in which our leaders recognize the problem and address it, moving beyond mere deficit cutting to reversing the loss of fiscal freedom—to restoring the power of today's and future generations to set their own course, shape their own destiny, and respond to the challenges before them in their own way.

In this world of our imagination—indeed, our hopes—the payoffs are sizable and profound. Each year that our economy grows, government revenues grow with it. That is because a growing economy generates more profits for businesses and higher incomes for households. If existing commitments no longer automatically claim those revenues and taxes start paying our bills, policymakers will have the fiscal freedom to assess the nation's current problems and address them more appropriately.

As the richest nation known to history, we clearly have the resources to address foreign threats, help the jobless return to work, and attack poverty more systematically. Most important, we have the resources to invest more robustly in our young—while keeping government lean enough that the economy can continue to grow.

Today, the average household produces an output (or, share of GDP) of more than $130,000 a year. Federal, state, and local spending, along with tax subsidies, now tops $55,000 a year per household. Back in 1980, the corresponding figures were about $87,000 a year in GDP and $30,000 in total spending and subsidies. Today the "direct support" that we provide for individuals—such as Social Security, Medicare, and SNAP (formerly known as food stamps)—alone tops $24,000 per household a year, and total social welfare, including education, tops $30,000. The poverty line in America is about $11,500 for an individual and $19,500 for a family of three. So, as a nation we already spend far more than necessary to give everyone incomes well above the poverty line, if we wanted to. That, alone, refutes the notion that we cannot do anything new or bold, or respond to new needs and emerging opportunities.

Moving forward, even below-average economic growth will generate within a few years trillions of dollars more in personal income. Within a decade, those rising incomes are projected to yield more than $1 trillion in additional annual revenues, even if tax rates fall a bit, and that is just the beginning of what the future will bring. Even if the twenty-first century does not bring growth rates that duplicate those of the twentieth (when per capita incomes grew eightfold), average output per household within the lifetime of a newborn baby will likely at least double or quadruple, and government's share of that output will rise from $55,000 to well more than $100,000 per household—regardless of whether government grows or shrinks as a share of GDP. No matter how you look at it, the possibilities before us seem extraordinary—if we remove the straightjacket from the fiscal freedom that would give us another shot at greatness.[5]

What we need is a government that can seize the moment and act with flexibility and vigor toward twenty-first century priorities and possibilities.

Overview of the Book

We did not reach this point overnight. The loss of fiscal freedom is the end result of decades of changes in Washington, rooted in altered visions about economic policy and the role of government to address economic and social ills. Failure to understand this history threatens our ability to move forward, often leaving us with some simplistic belief that it is only the stupidity of our opponents that reins us in. It is a complex story, with vast implications for our future—all of which I discuss in the pages that follow.

In Chapter 2, I explain that the nation has reached what I call a "fiscal turning point," marking a time when its structures and processes seem outdated and ill-equipped to address the challenges before it. The United States has faced at least two earlier fiscal turning points when it desperately needed the fiscal freedom to address the possibilities before it: during the Revolutionary Era, when the government established under the Articles of Confederation proved too weak even to pay our debts, prompting our founders to write a new Constitution; and at the start of the Progressive Era, when the nation's leaders began to add the governmental structures that proved necessary for an emerging world power. Each time, the nation's leaders were forced to acknowledge, and then to convince the public, that the existing fiscal structure was an impediment to national progress. To understand the concept of a fiscal turning point, I suggest viewing the budget not in traditional terms of spending and taxes but, instead, in terms of "giveaways" (tax cuts and spending increases) and "takeaways" (tax increases and spending cuts).

In Chapter 3, I trace the roots of our central problem—the loss of fiscal freedom. Starting in the 1930s, the federal government assumed a central role in ensuring the public's economic and social well-being. Economic theories like Keynesian and supply-side economics provided intellectual fuel for politicians to tolerate deficits on a regular basis and, thus, to compete with one another over which could provide more "giveaways" to voters. Policymakers in both parties grew increasingly active—viewing government as a key tool for solving not just economy-wide problems, but the problems of retirement, health care, education, poverty, and so on.

In Chapter 4, I describe the three distinct periods of fiscal policy since the end of World War II, each distinguished by the dominance of either "giveaways" or "takeaways." In the Era of Easy Finance, from 1945 to 1981, almost every major legislative action on fiscal policy came in the form of a tax cut or spending increase. Presidents and Congresses had the fiscal freedom to engage in activist domestic policy because they worked from a budget with few permanent commitments, with large "peace dividends" that accrued from post-war cuts in defense, and with automatic tax increases due to inflation that pushed people into higher tax brackets. In the Era of Fiscal Straightjackets, from 1982 to 1997, almost every major legislative action on fiscal policy consisted of tax increases and spending cuts to address surging deficits. By the late 1990s, surpluses replaced deficits due to earlier legislative action, a stock market bubble that generated an unexpected surge in revenues, a continued peace dividend from the end of the Cold War, a Democratic-Republican stalemate on major new giveaway legislation, and other factors. Finally, in the Era of Two Santas, from 1997 to 2010, policymakers ignored the temporary nature of those surpluses, threw caution to the wind, and became the most profligate generation of leaders in the nation's history. As the first decade of this new century drew to a close, a major global recession, the unprecedented profligacy of the Two-Santa Era, and the natural growth of retirement and health programs combined to create an enormous tidal wave of short- and long-run economic challenges both at home and abroad.

In Chapter 5, I detail how elected officials moved from battles over controlling the present to controlling the future. A few decades ago, most programs were temporary and almost none had built-in growth. Even a fairly activist government that was cutting taxes or increasing spending could stay on track to generate surpluses within a few years. Gradually, policymakers decided not just to enact permanent spending and tax programs, but also to boost the size of benefits and number of eligible recipients under them and, most importantly, to build automatic growth into them while keeping taxes low relative to those liabilities.

Several entitlement programs became automatically more generous from year-to-year, while policymakers made few adjustments for changing demographics — particularly fewer young workers to support all programs. Meanwhile, health programs remain open-ended, allowing doctors and patients to instigate ever more government spending on new and more expensive treatments.[6] Eventually spending growth would automatically exceed revenue growth.

In Chapter 6, I detail the four deadly economic consequences of our disease: (1) rising and unsustainable levels of debt, (2) the shrinking ability of policymakers to fight recession or address other emergencies, (3) a budget that invests ever less in our children and our future and is now a blueprint for a declining nation, and (4) a broken government, as reflected in antiquated tax and social welfare systems. These economic consequences all flow from the decades-long effort by each party to control the future by imposing its agenda on generations to come. By itself, short-term deficit cutting focuses almost solely on the first, but does little to solve even that problem. It can even exacerbate it by, for instance, weakening the economy in the near-term, or by short-changing investments in the future. By contrast, efforts to restore fiscal freedom will help address all of the deadly economic consequences of our current path.

In Chapter 7, I move from the economic consequences of this disease to its three deadly political consequences: (1) a decline of "fiscal democracy" as the loss of long-term budget balance deprives current and future voters of the right to control their own budget; (2) a classic "prisoner's dilemma," under which elected officials correctly conclude that they will threaten their own left-leaning or right-leaning agenda and also suffer politically if they lead efforts to impose spending cuts or tax hikes on their constituents; and (3) rising hurdles to changing our fiscal course because, to do anything new, officials must renege on past promises of rising benefits and low taxes that voters have come to expect. The longer we remain on our current course, the more such hurdles will grow, reinforcing partisanship and making a course correction ever more elusive.

In Chapter 8, I examine the coming counter-revolution by the forces of the status quo—the predictable effort to block the needed changes in programs and processes that would restore fiscal freedom for ourselves and future generations. Apologists for the status quo will deploy three sets of arguments, each of which centers on a legitimate concern that they will then take too far. They will argue that (1) we should focus on the size of government, not the issue of better government; (2) we should always increase, not reduce, the economic comfort, security, and certainty that government promises to the American people; and (3) excessive promises are not a problem since government can rewrite its laws whenever it chooses.

In Chapter 9, I return to the extraordinary possibilities that this fiscal turning point offers for creating twenty-first century government. Restoring fiscal freedom is about tapping the traditional "can-do" spirit of America. It is about taking a budget for a declining nation that invests ever less in our future and for a broken government that presides over archaic, inefficient, and inequitable spending and tax programs and converting it to one that confronts problems and seizes new possibilities. It is about creating a budget oriented toward investment, particularly for children, while recognizing the limits to the twentieth-century goal of providing ever higher levels of consumption that can negatively influence work, saving, and output. At the same time, restoring fiscal freedom is about creating a more adaptive government that abandons policies that do not work and readily redresses those programs that violate such basic principles as equal justice.

In Chapter 10, I return to lessons from past fiscal turning points. At those moments, reforms all had one crucial ingredient: they increased the fiscal freedom of policymakers. During the current fiscal turning point, freeing up the future requires fewer efforts to control it. As with earlier fiscal turning points, fundamental institutional and rule changes will be at the heart of this shift. We need a sweeping reform that removes permanent built-in deficits as only a first step toward changing Washington and restoring the future. It requires both parties to accept limits on policies that go too far in attempting to control the future, reinforced by changes that would make the budget process far more transparent to average Americans. Democrats would agree to limit the automatic growth that policymakers can build into major spending programs for health insurance, retirement security, and other key entitlements. Republicans would agree to do likewise for automatically growing tax subsidies and, except for recessions and emergencies, to set fiscal policy to generate the revenues needed to pay current bills rather than pass them off to future generations in the form of more debt. Government budget offices would report on the budget in more transparent ways, making clearer the responsibility of policymakers for all changes in spending and taxes—not just those newly enacted, but those they inherited from the past and allowed to remain in place. Once restored, fiscal freedom would free future voters to focus on the problems and opportunities of their own time, allowing them to decide better the size and nature of any governmental response.

2

At a Fiscal Turning Point

I am coming more and more to find that if a thing has not been done it is tremendously hard to get anyone today in favor of doing it.

—George Marshall

At its core, fiscal policy is about deciding what government should do, and how to finance it.

As a general matter, government cannot avoid political, economic, and social challenges. With the nation growing, the economy evolving, and society changing in all sorts of ways, policymakers must continually reform outdated processes of government so that the nation is empowered, not encumbered, to turn its attention to the challenges at hand.

At times, the continuing efforts to tinker with outdated processes are simply inadequate for the challenges that have emerged. At that moment, the United States reaches a "fiscal turning point"—a point that demands a significant revamping of the institutions and processes of government.[1] Here, still in the early years of a new century, the signs are unmistakable that the United States has reached just such a fiscal turning point.

The signs stretch from the economic to the political—legislative impasses, rising levels of partisanship, sequesters that cut programs in arbitrary ways, youth disaffection from established political parties of both left and right, threats to bring government to a halt, and rigid adherence to agendas established long ago and largely unresponsive to the challenges at hand. Clearly, the country must change not only the way that it conducts economic and social policy, but related governmental institutions and processes as well.

This is not America's first fiscal turning point. Major wars certainly led to radical and permanent restructurings of our fiscal landscape. More relevant for our purposes here are times less when government responded to crises with large fiscal change and more when fiscal regimes had clearly become antiquated, yet only with much anguish did the public and its government adjust to the large historical forces at play. Especially deserving of our attention are two cases when the lack of fiscal freedom threatened our long-term future. The first came during the early post-Revolutionary Era, when the government that had been established under the Articles of Confederation proved extraordinarily weak, prompting the founders to write a new Constitution and create a stronger government. A second came during the Progressive Era, when the nation's leaders added the governmental structures that proved necessary to compete with the rising power of nation-states abroad and industrial tycoons at home.[2]

To further understand how these two fiscal turning points relate to the current one, let us think about the federal budget in a new way. Normally, we think of the budget in terms of two sides—taxes on one side, spending on the other. For our purposes, let us think of it in other terms for the two sides—"giveaways" and "takeaways." With give-aways, policymakers provide benefits in the form of tax cuts and spending increases for politically favored groups and, at times, the population as a whole. With takeaways, they impose burdens in the form of tax increases or spending cuts on this or that group.[3] This different way of viewing the budget better reflects the reality of public policymaking.

Elected officials prefer to play Santa Claus, allocating giveaways about which they can brag to their constituents, nourishing their popularity and helping to ensure their reelection. Not surprisingly, they seek to avoid imposing (or at least hide) takeaways that raise the ire of constituents, reduce their popularity, and—worst of all—threaten their reelection. That political reality is as true in America today as it was a century or two ago, and it is as true in other electoral democracies around the world. It is the nature of the political beast, endemic to representative government.

What makes the previous two fiscal turning points relevant for today is that they each required elected officials to create new structures and processes that imposed takeaways that were large and explicit and would generate fierce public opposition. Because elected officials who acted would often pay the ultimate political price at election time, they were often reluctant to act, and delays in achieving fundamental reform imposed additional burdens on the public. Not surprisingly, the current turning point requires much the same focus and presents the same political threats and theatre to the elected officials of our time.

Post-Revolution: Defining Ourselves as a Nation

The new nation's first fiscal turning came with its founding. Most people do not think of the Revolutionary War much in financial terms but, in truth, we could not finance the war on our own, and we sent our most notable statesmen—Benjamin Franklin, John Adams, and Thomas Jefferson—to France in search of loans and support. At home, we borrowed heavily and relied significantly on the resources of the French armies and navies to bring the British to bay.

Even with borrowed funds from abroad, the Continental Congress had proven so inept at raising money that it consistently failed to pay even its often ragged and ill-fed troops. After hostilities ceased, American officers from the Continental Army gathered at Newburgh, New York and began talking of marching on the capital to get the back pay and pensions that were promised to them. George Washington was forced to help dissipate this threat. Addressing a group of angry and tired soldiers, he took a pair of reading glasses from his pocket, fumbled with them, and in a moment that reportedly moved some to tears declared, "Gentlemen, you will permit me to put on my spectacles, for I have not only grown gray but almost blind in the service of my country."[4]

A significant share of borrowing during the war was state borrowing but, under the Articles of Confederation, most of their debts and those of the confederation remained unpaid, and the debt was often sold at a discount. Even without those debts, success in war left the nation financially weak and without strong governing institutions; it could not finance the activities of a government appropriate for that era or meet the needs of a rapidly expanding population.[5]

Despite Americans' protests against British taxes, the taxes that their own democratically elected governments imposed on them immediately after the war were much higher than before the Revolutionary War. The main reason was war debts, which were about 75 to 80 percent of state government costs.[6] The national government lacked the power to impose taxes, and state governments were neither willing nor able to supply funds. Of the $13.7 million that Congress requested, the states raised only $5 million and, of that, $1.8 million were in bills that were unusable outside the United States.[7] To the extent that state governments were willing to raise taxes, tax collection during this founding period before a new Constitution was adopted was a laborious and uncertain process. Moreover, a government that was almost entirely devoted to paying off debts, even while its population was expanding rapidly westward and foreign threats remained serious, would not have enough revenue left to function.

We may think that we have serious opposition to taxes today, but in that earlier period, armed rebellions occasionally erupted, with one— Shays' Rebellion—compelling George Washington to come out of retirement and help guide the nation on a new course. While the tax revolts threatened disintegration, they also strengthened the resolve of those seeking a stronger national government. Forward-looking leaders of the time saw ways to convert this anarchy into a useful catalyst for action. They needed a way to raise enough revenue to pay off the debts and create a functioning government, without taxing to the point of inciting open revolt.

Thus, this first major debt crisis and related tax revolts became key driving forces in establishing a government that could serve an expanding nation well into the nineteenth century. It required drastic fiscal reforms. The first step was the Constitution, which gave new enumerated powers to a national government. Fights continued, however, over who would pay off state and national debts from the revolution, while citizens and foreign governments questioned the government's reliability to meet its obligations.

Just ten days after Treasury Secretary Alexander Hamilton took office in 1789, the House of Representatives asked him for a plan to address the national debt. No one expected him to try to pay the whole debt but, rather, only partly repay certificate holders what they were owed. That is because much of the original debt was sold to speculators, sometimes for only 1 to 30 percent of value.[8] Additionally, debt was held by a wide range of Americans, often in the form of written promises that dated back to the Revolution. Moreover, without a clear set of accounts, the true value of debts was obscured by faulty memories or outright lies.[9]

But Hamilton had his own plan. Not only did he propose to pay foreign debt (for which U.S. credibility was on the line overseas) in full, he also recommended paying the entire domestic debt as well—whether the holders were speculators or not.[10] Furthermore, he proposed that the federal government assume state debts because, he suggested, that would reduce financial uncertainty, allow for more uniform taxation, and perhaps even reduce the costs of administering the multiple sources of debt. Hamilton also believed that the federal government should establish predominance in the fiscal sphere. For Congress, that was a particularly controversial idea; Northern states tended to have much higher debts, leading the Southern states to cry foul. The ultimate compromise, ironed out by Hamilton, Jefferson, and Madison, required that the federal government assume state debts and, in exchange for Southern generosity on that front, that the nation's capital be moved to the South—to the new city of Washington, D.C.[11]

Hamilton still had an enormous problem, however—how to do what he promised. A broke federal government now had to pay a $54 million debt (on top of an additional $25 million from the states).[12] This plan included other major features, including greater federal borrowing powers, a new national tariff, and a stronger Treasury Department. To mitigate direct taxation, the federal government managed to convert debt into long-term securities, which it could pay back at a slower rate with reduced interest. Most important, the plan established the federal government as a higher fiscal power than the states. None of these moves was terribly popular. But the public acquiesced, accepting a greater centralization of power in exchange for a government that would start to serve their needs.

Leadership mattered. As Bruce Davie, a public finance expert, wrote, "Hamilton viewed the debt not so much as a problem but as both an economic and political opportunity"—and he made the most of it.[13] He realized, for example, that by giving government debt credibility, he could turn bonds into a legitimate part of the money supply and supplement the scarce supply of coin currency. He also understood that by assuming state debts, he gave debt holders a reason to want a government that was strong enough to make reliable payments, giving the merchant class an investment in the federal government.

To be sure, this new fiscal regime had its costs. Tariffs, which became the major new source of revenues, were a clever way to hide the burden of taxation from most Americans: people paid for tariffs in the form of more expensive goods, but this was less obvious than direct taxation. Not everyone was happy with the tariffs, either. They were quite inequitable, tending to protect Northeastern manufacturers at the expense of Southerners who bore much of their burden through higher prices. Meanwhile, Westerners who often supported the new infrastructure that the tariffs financed nevertheless distrusted Eastern powers and bankers.

In a democracy, politics normally reflects larger forces at work across society. Change brings turmoil and, when turmoil breeds public unhappiness, it shifts power among political parties. Not surprisingly, the new tariffs helped weaken the Federalist Party, reducing its support in the South and West so much that it never regained the presidency after 1800 and faded away over the next two decades. The fiscal reforms that the Federalists had enacted years earlier, however, empowered the government and enabled the country to progress—to pay our bills at home, borrow from abroad, and become a trusted partner in international trade.

As the economy grew, the tariffs and other taxes that the Federalists put in place grew with it, generating more and more federal revenues every year. These revenues gave policymakers the fiscal freedom and resources not just to finance the basic operations of government, but also to underwrite what Henry Clay would call the "American system"—the combination of tariffs, banking, roads, canals, and internal improvements that helped develop profitable markets for agriculture and fuel westward expansion.

Less recognized, the freedom associated with this new fiscal infrastructure allowed policymakers to cut taxes on occasion and, fortunately, convinced Americans to express their views toward their government through the ballot box rather than by force of arms. Not long after the federal government had raised taxes to assume state debts, taxes began to fall. Policymakers cut what had been an average tariff of more than 15 percent in 1791 to between 8 and 10 percent between 1795 and 1800.[14]

The new fiscal infrastructure did not bring armed tax revolts to a complete end. In the 1790s, farmers in what was then the western frontier used violence to prevent federal officials from collecting a tax on corn that was converted to whiskey, prompting George Washington to become the only sitting president ever to lead an army—a militia of 15,000 men—to suppress the insurrection. The tax, however, fueled support for the opposition party of Thomas Jefferson, which repealed the tax soon after Jefferson was elected president in 1800.

The Progressive Era: Response to the New Industrial Order

Another fiscal turning point began at the end of the nineteenth century, although its related fiscal reforms stretched well into the first decades of the twentieth. Those subsequent reforms are largely associated with what is called the Progressive Era, stretching from the presidency of Teddy Roosevelt to at least that of Woodrow Wilson.

At the start of that period, a relatively small federal government presided over a budget that was largely devoted to paying benefits to Civil War veterans and running the postal service.[15] From 1880 to 1910, over a quarter of non-postal spending was devoted to pensions for veterans— an amount that exceeded or nearly equaled every other major category of spending, other than interest payments on the national debt.[16]

Once again, our federal government, this time facing new challenges presented by global economic forces and America's emergence as a world power, was not up to the tasks before it. Progress in manufacturing, communication, and even war-making—based largely on economies of scale—brought prospects of advancement. If nothing else, simply financing government's grander activities, such as the building of the Panama Canal (a once-floundering French project over which the United States took control in 1904), demanded a government of greater size and scope.

The world was changing, and the nation was changing with it— swiftly. A country that had spent more than a century exploring, conquering, and populating the barren lands to its West shifted its focus.[17] The economy moved from agriculture to manufacturing, and Americans increasingly moved from farms to cities that were already teeming with millions of new immigrants who had come to America's shores throughout the nineteenth century. Workers, who faced harsh working conditions in factories and other settings, increasingly organized themselves into unions, launching strikes against major businesses that, in a growing economy, could have adverse effects far beyond the gates of a single business or the borders of a single city.

The federal government faced growing pressures to protect workers from the ravages of industrialization, to enable businesses to better compete, and to ensure that the United States could take its rightful place on the international stage. These were national challenges, transcending state borders and involving America's place in the world, and they demanded a response by a federal government that would have to assume new responsibilities.

Like the earlier fiscal turning point, this one, too, involved its own fiscal crises. In 1897, federal debt soared due to a poor economy, bloated Civil War pensions, and rising spending for debt service and public improvements. President William McKinley turned to the traditional method of raising revenue—raising tariffs. Duties reached an average of 57 percent, and the burden that the most highly taxed items imposed on consumers prompted populists such as William Jennings Bryan to attack the tariff as unfair to the average American. Many began to fear that tariffs were high enough to undercut the abilities of American companies to sell goods abroad by preventing Europeans from selling goods in America. Thus, even the traditionally protectionist Republicans had reason to protest the new tariffs. A new tariff law reduced imports but did little to solve government's fiscal problems.[18]

In response to these teeming forces and the new demands and possibilities they entailed, the nation launched a second set of dramatic structural reforms: a new income tax that would gradually replace the tariff and provide a base for raising significant revenues, a new Federal Reserve System to regulate monetary policy and develop a national banking strategy, and new regulatory structures to reduce the power of monopolies and promote a competitive economy.

As in the earlier fiscal turning point, the stakes for vested interests again were high, so the struggles were fierce. The government would be taking power and money from one set of groups while providing more power and protection to others. The battles would pit region against region, class against class, agriculture against industry. Teddy Roosevelt's antitrust war with industrial "robber barons" was so fierce that, while he was traveling to Africa after his presidency, the industrialist J.P. Morgan reportedly toasted, "America expects every lion to do its duty!" (Another version of the story has Morgan wishing "Health to the lions.")[19]

The battles of that period dragged on for some time. The Supreme Court ruled in 1895[20] that the income tax that President Grover Cleveland and Congress had enacted a year earlier was unconstitutional, prompting lawmakers to draft the Sixteenth Amendment to the Constitution, which was finally ratified in 1913. Not surprisingly, many industrialists fiercely opposed the new tax. They had benefited from tariffs and government subsidies; they would now pay taxes.[21]

The institutions and processes that policymakers created during the Progressive Era have proven enormously flexible and resilient. The Federal Reserve System survives to this day and dominates monetary policy. Antitrust policy has a mixed record in coping with modern forms of market power but, supplemented by the Federal Trade Commission, it still acts at times on behalf of consumers and polices large mergers— today more likely to be airlines or telecommunications than steel or railroads. The income tax—never fully popular, in no small part due to its visibility—continues to dominate the nation's tax structure; America's leaders expanded it to finance U.S. participation in World War I, kept it alive in contracted form between the wars, and expanded it enormously to finance U.S. participation in World War II.

Like the fiscal turning at the nation's beginning, this one, too, was followed by reforms that gave policymakers significant fiscal freedom to operate effectively in a new century. Revenues would grow with the economy and in most years give policymakers choices over what to do with much of those revenues. The fiscal freedom allowed policymakers both to expand programs and cut taxes at times. In recent decades, lawmakers have cut the top tax rate dramatically, but other changes in tax rates and an expanded base on which taxes are imposed has enabled the government to collect about the same share of the nation's income since World War II.

Once again, the swirl of economic and social change, and the demands for a government to address the new challenges, generated profound political upheaval across the late nineteenth and early twentieth centuries. The Republican Party, which had mostly dominated U.S. politics in the late nineteenth century, split early in the twentieth. Roosevelt returned from retirement in 1912 to mount a "Bull Moose" challenge to incumbent Republican Howard Taft, promising a more vigorous federal government to regulate business and protect ordinary people better than the more conservative Taft had done over the previous four years. The split among Republicans—Roosevelt received 27 percent of the vote, while Taft garnered 23 percent—paved the way for victory by Democrat Woodrow Wilson.

Wilson, the former Princeton University president and New Jersey governor, took full advantage of the opportunity, building on earlier Republican reforms and presiding over U.S. entry into, and victory in, World War I. But, by 1920, Americans had tired of the crusades to better humanity at home and abroad and returned the White House to the Republicans. Their successful candidate, Warren G. Harding, had promised "not nostrums but normalcy."[22] Yet, even with Republicans in power under Harding, Coolidge, and Hoover over the next dozen years, policymakers maintained the progressive income tax, albeit at significantly reduced rates from its wartime highs.

Like our first fiscal turning point, the second was driven by the need to address governmental inadequacy as well as the potential pay-off for doing so. The first turning point was largely driven by the need to pay old debt and sell new debt, create a banking system, and establish taxing powers. The second further strengthened the government's power to raise revenue and regulate the economy, planting the seeds of government's dramatic growth in ensuing decades.

No change of this magnitude could be perfect and, in fact, government's expansions in our first two fiscal turning points created their own sets of problems, including repeated episodes of corruption, waste, and excessive planning and regulation. The larger the government, the greater was the opportunity for public officials to steer federal dollars to their friends or, worse, stick their own hands in the cookie jar to claim some of the federal largesse for themselves.

In the early nineteenth century, Henry Clay (among others) received kick-backs from Nicholas Biddle, the corrupt president of the Second Bank of the United States. The tariffs of that period, meanwhile, largely served domestic manufacturers who could get the highest tariff rates, while the road, railroad, and other construction activities that they supported often went to those with the most political connections and money. As for the Progressive Era, the larger governments that it presaged set the stage for more lobbying and influence peddling in Washington, with corporate interests in particular positioned to confront new taxes and regulation while carving out more subsidies for their businesses.

Nevertheless, whatever the problems with the particular reforms, government fiscal policy had to change. "History had moved on," as the oxymoron goes. Reform was inextricably driven by a serious mismatch between on the one hand the changing needs of the nation, an evolving economy, and a restless people; and, on the other, a government of each era that lacked the authority, the tools, and the flexibility to respond accordingly. Something had to be done, and so it was.

Something must be done once more.

Today: Pursuing the Past

At today's fiscal turning point, we again find our government inadequate to address the challenges at hand. The world is changing at breakneck speed, with the economy growing more globalized, international competition becoming ever-more fierce, jobs requiring ever-greater levels of skills, our people growing older, inequality rising, cash incomes stagnant for many middle-income Americans, and poverty proving stubbornly persistent. Yet, we find that essentially all government resources have been committed not just for today, but for the twenty-first century and beyond—largely through decades-old and inconsistent visions of spending and tax priorities that failed to address or adapt to many of these problems.

Huge deficits, especially after the Great Recession of 2007–09, have shown America and much of the developed world that change is necessary, but they mask the broader implications of this fiscal turning point. Even the boldest attempts by deficit reduction commissions, such as President Obama's "Simpson-Bowles" Commission, typically aim for bare fiscal sustainability and still leave all or almost all revenues committed by the actions of dead and past legislators. The fiscal democracy index (described in the previous chapter) still heads toward zero. Smaller and arbitrary efforts to cut spending across the board (for example, through sequestration) provide no principled guidance for how to reform programs or reallocate dollars.

Deficit reduction agreements may be necessary, but they are not sufficient to create a government for the new century. Deficit reduction can no more set out an agenda for successful government today than could paying off Revolutionary War debt over two hundred years ago. Yes, we might want to go there but, upon arriving, as Gertrude Stein might have said, "there is no there there."

We need a government that can respond effectively to today's multiplicity of challenges—to create structures and systems that will invest better in our children, rein in soaring health care costs while extending health care coverage to those who lack it, promote the educational progress of every student from very young age to adulthood, invest in those who are pursuing higher education and those who are not, better employ and engage the unemployed and people with disabilities, address the challenge of an unusually underemployed young adult population, invest in basic research, and modernize our infrastructure.

Yet, we also want to do all this in a way that keeps government lean and leaves most decision-making in the hands of the citizens of tomorrow, not the elected officials or bureaucrats of yesterday.

Better government is not the only answer but, along with the cooperation of a host of important players in the private sector that include business, labor, and charitable and academic communities, it is surely one of the necessary answers. Nor is the answer simply a bigger government. This fiscal turning point shares with the other two examined here an extraordinary need for a new level of flexibility.

But, that is not because we lack the basic fiscal structures of government, as we did at the nation's beginning, nor because we have a government with all-too-limited powers, as we did as we moved into the industrial age. This time, the problem is the extraordinary level of permanent and growing commitments we have made to existing spending programs and tax subsidies, and the parallel promise not to collect enough revenues to pay for it all. No matter how much the economy might grow in the future, all future revenues are already committed to permanent programs established by past legislators—to the exclusion of everything else.

Of particular concern is the failure to adjust for rising health costs and a demographic shift without parallel in history. These affect the budget not only through ever-rising and unsustainable levels of health and retirement benefits, but also through related reductions in revenues due to a population with smaller shares of working adults.

At the same time, so many other spending benefits and tax subsidies have a permanent status that, regardless of their built-in growth, they, too, tend to pre-empt any rational reordering of government toward current needs and opportunities.

Worse, we are reluctant to raise revenues to cover today's spending, much less to finance the even costlier commitments to the future that we have made. Future generations are left not only with unsustainable promises but also with the leftover bills from previous generations who never paid their own way.

To be clear, when it comes to social welfare programs, more security is usually a good thing. Elected officials who created and then expanded many government programs and tax subsidies sought to respond to real public needs, whether that was a large share of elderly Americans who were living in poverty or the large share of Americans of all ages who lacked health insurance.

The issue, then, is one of balance—of balancing, on the one hand, the desire to provide ever greater security and, on the other, the need for a government that has the flexibility to respond to the challenges of the future that, by definition, we cannot foresee. No business or family seeking security would do what our government has done—commit itself on how exactly to spend all of its future hoped-for revenues. No business or family would do what else our government has done—make formal commitments it cannot possibly meet. Finally, no business or family would establish a budget that in essence precludes its youth from setting new priorities when they become adults.

To address the problem, we must do more than reduce the levels of debt that, under current policies, will continue to rise faster than our national income. We must restore flexibility to our government and enable our leaders to allocate future resources to future needs, not just to cover previous commitments. In essence, we must enable our future by trying to control it less.

Specifically, we must be willing to do three things:

- remove the automatic and eternal built-in growth in programs that current policies will generate—not because they will fail to meet some social goal but, instead, because their current claim for ever-more of our future dollars will mean less and less for other, potentially more worthwhile, endeavors;
- pay our bills in normal economic times and stop pretending that deficit-financed tax cuts do anything more than shift burdens onto our children; and
- start using some of the resources that we free up from steps (1) and (2), above, to invest wisely in our children, in programs devoted more to opportunity and mobility than ever-more consumption, in our future more broadly, and in what works—giving us a government that is not only more effective but far leaner than the one that our current course will generate.[23]

We must let future Americans adjust tax and spending levels according to the needs of their time, without trying to pre-ordain their future. That requires balance: if we should not allow past commitments to claim all future revenues, so too should we not allow today's leaders to place extraordinary limits (such as eternal "no-new-tax" pledges or super-majority voting requirements) on the allowable levels of taxes that tomorrow's public will pay.

Why are both parties so reluctant to do this? Because it would jeopardize their future-controlling agendas. For today's elected officials, the task at hand is particularly threatening. As in previous fiscal turnings, they would need to ask voters to give up something to create a more effective government and a stronger economy for themselves and their children.

3

From Whence It Came

The modern era has been dominated by the culminating belief that the world . . . is a wholly knowable system governed by finite number of universal laws that man can grasp and rationally direct . . . objectively describing, explaining, and controlling everything.

—Vaclav Havel,
Czechoslovakia's first president after the Soviet Union fell

To reduce the extraordinary power of past policymakers over future spending and tax policy, and to restore the fiscal freedom required for any government to capitalize on new opportunities, we have a very big job ahead of us. We must do more than reduce deficits and debt to sustainable levels. We must free up public resources so we can address the challenges to come while leaving government fit enough to do its job well.

The roots of our current challenge are two-fold. First, Keynesian and then supply side theory, while initially designed to address legitimate economic concerns, eventually provided the intellectual fuel to politicians for almost any spending increase, tax cut, and resulting deficit.

Parts of this chapter have appeared previously in Lawrence J. Haas, "Understanding What's Driving the Annual Deficit," in *Governing to Win: Enhancing National Competitiveness Through New Policy and Operating Approaches,* ed. Charles L. Prow (Lanham: Rowman & Littlefield Publishers, Inc., 2012) and in C. Eugene Steuerle, "Fiscal Democracy or Why Sound Fiscal Policy, Budget Consolidation and Inclusive Growth Require Fewer, Not More, Attempts to Control the Future," in *Promoting Inclusive Growth: Challenges and Policies,* ed. Luiz de Mello and Mark A. Dutz (Paris, OECD Publishing, 2012), 147–76.

Second, growing public expectations that the federal government should address economic and social hardship stimulated a decades-long growth in the federal bureaucracy and in the related network of private trade groups, think tanks, policy advocates, and lobbyists that at times bolster unreasonable expectations for more federal activism. These forces date back to the 1930s, forming an important prelude to the decline in fiscal democracy.

For several decades now, Democrats and Republicans have used Keynesian and supply side theories, respectively, to justify ever-more types of government efforts to steer the economy and address social problems. In doing so, they increasingly locked in automatically growing domestic programs and low tax rates as far into the future as possible—with limited regard for whether the programs were right for a rapidly evolving world and how to cover their ever-growing costs. In competing with one another to control the future, both parties deprived future generations of their right to use government to respond to their own challenges and shape their own future.

Not long after the turn into the twenty-first century, the unsustainable deficits and debt that were increasingly fueled by those automatically growing spending programs and low taxes were brought to a head and then exacerbated by the Great Recession, the financial crisis, and the extraordinary steps that policymakers took to address them. By the second decade of the new century, policymakers at last turned their attention to the rising red ink, but largely sidestepped the roots of the problem, relying instead on budgetary gimmicks such as sequestration or across-the-board cuts in a selected list of programs, without any regard to need or priority.

When it came to the real dollars at stake, Democrats remained unwilling to sacrifice their support for permanently growing retirement and health programs and Republicans remained unwilling to rethink their commitment to maintain taxes that were far too low to finance the permanent spending. In essence, policymakers sought to have it both ways—to express their commitment to lower deficits and debt, but with no interest in addressing the fundamental drivers of that problem.

What neither party has been offering, of course, is any vision for shaping a twenty-first century America that would retain its leadership role in the world and address the challenges of a more globalized economy, of jobs that demand more education and skills, of an aging

population, of an inadequate educational system, of an antiquated infrastructure, and so on. Neither party was offering a vision for how to
free up resources to address future recessions, natural disasters, terrorist
attacks, or the challenges that we cannot anticipate.

The American Aversion to Debt

"Deficits don't matter," Vice President Dick Cheney famously told Treasury Secretary Paul O'Neill when, during President George W. Bush's
first term, O'Neill raised concerns that a second big tax cut would generate big new budget deficits.[1]

It was a striking moment, but one that was a long time in coming.
Indeed, the transformation of fiscal policy—from the rigid balanced
budget orthodoxy that had dominated policymaking for most of the
nation's history to Cheney's disregard for growing deficits in the early
twenty-first century—began in the 1930s with the reasonable Keynesian
notion that deficits may be not only acceptable but even beneficial to
help boost a struggling economy. The notion gathered steam in ensuing
decades, however, to justify deficits under most circumstances.

An American aversion to debt dates back to the nation's founding.[2] "The question whether one generation of men has a right to bind
another," Thomas Jefferson suggested to James Madison,

> is a question of such consequences as not only to merit decision,
> but place also among the fundamental principles of every govern-
> ment. . . . I set out on this ground, which I suppose to be self-
> evident, "that the earth belongs in usufruct [the beneficial holding
> of property that ultimately belongs to another] to the living."[3]

James Madison was reportedly a man who could not utter the word
"debt" without also uttering "evil."

Controversies over U.S. debt date back to the Revolutionary War.
During the war mobilization, currency was scarce and the government
funded the war largely through bills of credit. Benjamin Franklin noted
the benefits of debt, writing in a letter to Samuel Cooper in 1779, "when
we are obligated to issue a Quantity excessive, it pays itself off in depreciation." More than any lack of confidence in a paper currency, it was
the overwhelming supply of bills of credit that devalued them. These
unpaid debts led to a major fiscal crisis for the fledgling United States,

as the young nation's leaders debated whether the debt of the individual states should be repaid and, if so, by who—the states themselves, or the federal government on their behalf.

Under Hamilton's guidance, the United States developed a plan to address its Revolutionary War debts. Hamilton was less worried about debt than about the government's institutional ability to handle it. He wanted a stronger national government that lenders, both at home and abroad, would consider credit-worthy. Not surprisingly, the level of debt would fluctuate with circumstances. Conflicts with Native Americans, tax revolts, tensions with France, and another war with England drove the debt up.

Despite his aversion to debt, Jefferson showed his pragmatic side when he borrowed the funds needed for the Louisiana Purchase in 1803, doubling the size of the United States. During Jefferson's re-election campaign a year later, the opposition Federalists attacked him over the rising debt. Treasury Secretary Albert Gallatin worked to bring it under control and make the government's finances more transparent, and he urged Congress to cut spending. "I know of but one way that a nation has of paying her debts; and this is precisely the same which individuals practice," Gallatin said. "Spend *less* than you receive."

Under President Andrew Jackson in 1835, the federal government fully repaid the national debt for the first time in U.S. history. Jackson called the debt a "curse," believing it gave power to a wealthy upper-class. Jackson's success resulted from not just his personal views but also from the fiscal discipline of past presidents and a tariff that grew rapidly with expanding commerce and population; in fact, tariff revenues grew even after policymakers cut its rate from time to time. The debt reappeared under Jackson due to a depression that he helped cause with his economic policies and his decision to close the national bank. The ensuing battle between the political parties over who was responsible for the debt's return reflected public aversion to debt and public determination to reduce it whenever possible.

For most of U.S. history, the federal government followed a clear pattern on the debt. Policymakers let the debt rise during wartime (when government needed to finance the military) or during economic slowdowns (when revenues fell), and they offset that debt by running surpluses during times of peace and prosperity. "Before the Great Depression," the historian John Steele Gordon, writes, "balancing the budget and paying down the debt were considered second only to the defense of the country as an obligation of the federal government."[4] From the nation's founding through 1932, the government ran 48 deficits, offset by 93 surpluses.[5]

The balanced budget orthodoxy that prevailed until the 1930s was buttressed by two basic factors.

First, political leaders and economists viewed balanced budgets as morally right and economically beneficial. Not only were balanced budgets mandated by state constitutions, they were revered at the federal level as an unwritten constitutional rule, constraining the nation's leaders.

Second, until the New Deal, the federal government in peacetime was tiny compared to today's behemoth, with far fewer activities, far fewer departments and agencies, and far fewer federal workers. The government ran few permanent programs other than a few tax breaks, and no spending program was scheduled to grow automatically and forever.[6] President Hoover had a professional staff of only four, and a 1929 Washington correspondent complained even about this "excessive number," noting that, "In bygone days, the President had one secretary . . . now there is a whole machine-gun squad to handle the work."[7]

"Blessed are the young for they shall inherit the national debt," President Herbert Hoover said, reflecting his aversion to it. Nevertheless, circumstances intervened on his watch to send deficits and debt rising. Revenues fell due to a sinking economy and deflation, while domestic spending rose substantially, especially as a percent of the economy (see Appendix).[8] Reflecting traditional attitudes, Roosevelt ran against Hoover by promising to balance the budget.

To be sure, spending rose during Roosevelt's New Deal. Much of the deficit on his watch, however, was due to a drop in revenues from a sick economy and high unemployment. FDR tried to reduce deficits, especially when it looked like the economy was growing stronger, and some later blamed his tax increases for sending the economy back into recession in the late 1930s.

Not until America's entry into World War II did Roosevelt launch massive deficit spending, generating debt that, as a share of the economy, was far greater than anything in our history.[9] The huge growth in wartime employment helped end the Great Depression, and much of the New Deal spending, which was largely temporary in nature and designed to help the unemployed, ended with it. Policymakers raised taxes substantially, and they would never again return to their prior lower levels.

The Arrival of the Keynesians

The Depression ushered in a period of monumental change in fiscal policy, upending the status quo. For starters, economist John Maynard Keynes enunciated a fiscal policy that, while not accepted as dogma until decades later, began to break the balanced budget shackle. He argued that governments should pursue deficit-financed stimulus measures in an economic downturn and, while he has since become a bête noir for today's economists of the right, even some of his early critics from the conservative "Chicago school of economics" had long ago concluded that budget balancing did not make sense during downturns.

To be sure, Keynesian economics also urged policymakers to do just the opposite during prosperity—that is, run surpluses. In later years, leading economists adopted Keynesianism as a general approach while amending the particulars.

Keynesians were never successful in developing a disciplining rule that had the force of the old balanced budget rule. They talked of balancing the budget over the business cycle or balancing the budget except for the debt caused by less-than-full employment, but such rules never caught on.

As much as anyone, it was Walter Heller, President John F. Kennedy's top economic adviser, who instilled government policy with the notion of stimulating the economy through tax cuts. The Kennedy tax cuts—some of which were enacted under his successor, Lyndon Johnson—represented the first major effort to stimulate the economy with a formal nod to Keynes, and the first successful effort to cut taxes permanently, as opposed to increasing spending temporarily, when the budget was already in deficit.

Nevertheless, Heller, too, worried about the economic cycle as a whole. While he pushed for Keynesian tax cuts in the early 1960s, he later advocated a tax increase during the Vietnam era to reduce deficits and avoid their potential inflationary effects. Charged with inconsistency, he replied, "I blow on my hands to warm them up. That doesn't keep me from blowing on my soup to cool it down."[10]

Not surprisingly, deficits proved contagious. As politicians accepted the notion that deficit spending was not only tolerable but actually beneficial during times of economic weakness, they proved less inclined to enact tax increases and spending cuts once the economy had recovered. The economy always seemed to be growing at too slow a rate or on the verge of the next recession. Outside of wartime tax increases that Congress enacted during World War II and the Korean War, which only partly offset the costs of those military endeavors, Congress enacted only one significant tax *rate* increase on Keynesian grounds—the temporary Vietnam-related surtax in 1968—only as part of a package of longer-term tax cuts. (The rare tax rate increase in 2013 under President Obama came during recovery from a recession and then only as an extension of a tax rate cut for most Americans that would not extend to the wealthy.)

Even while supporting the Keynesian notion of countercyclical fiscal policy, some leading tax experts began to worry about the implications for both tax policy and deficits. Leading Treasury economists and lawyers, like Carl Shoup, Roy Blough, and Stanley Surrey, feared that too much tinkering with the tax code would start to draw attention away from its main purpose: to finance government.[11] That concern did not get much attention in the 1960s and 1970s when tax cuts grew not just increasingly popular but also affordable. As the economy grew and inflation pushed taxpayers into higher tax brackets, revenues rose considerably from year to year. Policymakers could return some of those revenues to voters in the form of tax cuts.

Presidents Gerald Ford and Jimmy Carter worked with Congress to cut taxes in 1975, 1976, 1977, and 1978. The main issue that policymakers of that period faced was how big the tax cut should be. As it turns out, they were not big enough. The automatic tax increases that taxpayers faced largely because of very high inflation more than offset the tax cuts that policymakers enacted, adding momentum to a tax revolt that swelled by the end of the decade.

Then Came the Supply-Siders

By the time President Ronald Reagan took office in 1981, Keynesianism was a tarnished theory due to the stagflation—the combination of inflation and stagnation—of the mid-to-late 1970s. The Reagan team brought a renewed focus on monetary policy as a key tool to address short-run economic cycles. Reagan stood behind Federal Reserve Chairman Paul Volcker as the latter sought to wring inflation out of the economy by severely tightening the money supply, sending interest rates and unemployment skyward.

Nevertheless, Reagan wanted to—indeed, had promised to—provide a huge giveaway in the form of an across-the-board tax cut (while also proposing to build up defense and to cut domestic spending to partially offset all these costs). He and his acolytes needed an economic justification for the tax-cutting, and it came in the form of supply-side economics.

At its most basic level, supply-side economics stresses that on the "supply side"—that is, when workers decide whether to work and households decide whether to save—incentives matter. Higher tax rates affect behavior, even as experts debate by just how much. In particular, supply-siders stressed one aspect of these incentives—the higher the tax rate, the greater is the distortion from each percentage point increase in that rate.

To see why, think of a tax rate increase from 10 percent to 20 percent on all of your income. That additional ten percentage points would take away one-ninth of the income on which you formerly had to live (the additional 10 percent tax on the previously un-taxed 90 percent). Now, think of a tax rate increase from 90 percent to 100 percent that takes away all of the money you had formerly been allowed to keep.

From the government's standpoint, each ten-percentage-point increase would generate the same amount of additional revenues if your earnings did not change. But that is not the real world. If your tax rate rose from 10 percent to 20 percent, you might work less because you gain less from the work, but you might work more to make up for the lost income. If, however, your tax rate rose from 90 to 100 percent, you would gain nothing from working harder, so you would likely give up working altogether.

From World War II until the early 1960s, the top tax rate on individuals was 90 percent. Almost no one paid taxes at that rate, however, because high-income Americans avoided it in a variety of ways, such as through special breaks for capital gains or earning income through a corporation where the top rate was lower. Still, lots of people considered the rate onerous, not the least of whom was Reagan, who remembered facing the 90 percent rate when he was earning big bucks as a Hollywood actor.

But populist supply-siders—as opposed to legitimate scholars who decried the disincentives that high tax rates cause without over-stating the problem—wanted a seemingly endless stream of tax cuts, always promoting their benefits while ignoring their costs. For several decades now, the *Wall Street Journal's* editorial page has served as a public bulletin board for supply-side advocacy, providing the intellectual ammunition for Republican candidates to win elections through the promise of tax cutting. Problems ensued not when supply-side advocates discussed the issue of disincentives but, instead, when they outlined extraordinary benefits that debt-driven lower rates would purportedly generate both for the economy and, in particular, the federal fisc.

The *Journal,* moreover, pushed the argument almost no matter where tax rates or government deficits were at any point. It labeled the Reagan-era notion of across-the-board tax cuts a modest program, touted the economic benefits of rate cuts two decades later when President George W. Bush cut rates much lower than Reagan, and asserted in 2010 that higher taxes would not reduce the deficit, but instead weaken the economy.[12] Along the way, it attacked various nonpartisan government offices for not supporting its claims.

To be sure, tax cuts may actually pay for themselves when tax rates are very high, such as when the top tax rate is, say, 90 percent and policymakers reduce it significantly. That is because many people who would not work extra for the promise of keeping just 10 percent of their earnings might well work more if they could keep much more than that. But, this extreme version of the theory makes little sense when rates are lower—when, for instance, policymakers propose to cut the top tax rate from 39.6 percent (where it is at this writing) to, say, 30 or 25 percent.[13]

As with Keynesian theory, the basic insight of supply-side theory is sound. Taxes distort and they cause losses to the public. In the end, taxes are justified only if they finance spending that produces enough gains for society to offset both the direct tax costs and the extra costs from the distortions. So, in mulling tax hikes or tax cuts, policymakers must consider the particular circumstances and weigh benefits against costs. But, as with more politically minded advocates of Keynesian theory, the more politically minded supply siders want a "free lunch." They only want to talk about the economic advantages of tax cuts, not their cost in the form of higher deficits.[14]

Tax cuts that are financed by deficits involve a shifting of burdens, not their removal. Think of it this way: a tax cut financed by deficits is like borrowing by parents who use the money, then pass the additional debt on to their children to pay back at some future date. Only in special circumstances when the gains for the children from the use of that money more than compensate for the additional debt might it be said to be "free."

The economic twists and turns of the mid-to-late twentieth century, then, helped to nurture a policy world that, across political lines, was ever-more sympathetic to, or at least tolerant of, deficits. Keynesian stimulus and supply-side incentive arguments helped both parties move away from discussions of budget balancing each year or over the economic cycle, or of offsetting the costs of deficit increases with later spending cuts or tax increases.

As the twenty-first century dawned, President George W. Bush and his team suggested that his tax cuts were, simultaneously, good Keynesian stimulus to revive the economy from the 2001 recession and good supply-side-ism that would boost growth and revenues through the magic of low tax rates.[15] Driven by a first round of tax cuts (along with more spending for both domestic and defense purposes), the surpluses that Bush had inherited in early 2001 soon turned to deficits. But, Bush and congressional Republicans pushed for more tax cuts (and other defense and entitlement spending), as if oblivious to the rising red ink and their own pro-spending policies.

President Barack Obama followed that by pushing a large stimulus measure comprised of tax cuts and more spending through Congress in the midst of a deep recession in early 2009. During his "Fiscal Responsibility Summit" in late February of 2009, he pledged to cut the deficit in half by the end of his term, identified entitlements as the main driver of rising debt, and committed to health reform (as well as reforms for Social Security and the tax code). Yet, he did not offer any plan for fully addressing these challenges. He would leave that for future deliberation.[16]

The world had changed. Every fight over the budget or taxes now would confront Keynesian and supply-side theories that, when carried to extremes, favored those politicians who sought only to give something away, not take something back to balance the budget. The push for giveaways, often arbitrarily distributed, also came at the cost of decreased attention to fairness and efficiency in tax or spending policy.[17]

For elected officials, cutting taxes and increasing spending are, well, fun. They enable politicians to cater to their constituents by offering giveaways, boosting their popularity and improving their reelection prospects. The more fun, the more contagious that it all became. The more contagious, the more that politicians sought economic reasons—real or imagined—to support their actions. Those who tried to stand in the way—to protect the budget from unaffordable tax cuts or spending hikes—were dismissed as eat-your-spinach cranks.[18]

The Path We Have Taken

So, Keynesianism and supply-side-ism laid the economic predicate for more frequent deficits. Meanwhile, the growing activism of both political parties to achieve their economic and social goals through government was another key driving factor.

How did we get here?

Before 1933, the executive branch consisted of ten departments—State, Navy, War (later converted into Defense), Justice, Agriculture, Commerce, Labor, Treasury, Interior, and the Post Office.

While the Progressive Era marked a clear fiscal turning point that ushered in many of the basic structures of twentieth-century government, the government in 1900 still measured only about 2 percent of GDP, not much different from other Western nations. Soon after, however, government started responding much more vigorously to twentieth-century crises—first on the military side during World War I, then on the domestic side during the Great Depression. Almost immediately after taking office in early 1933, President Franklin Delano Roosevelt scrapped his balanced-budget promise and launched a rescue program for his economically desperate nation, dramatically expanding the size of government. Spending, which totaled 3 percent of gross domestic product in 1930, swelled under Roosevelt to 11 percent of GDP by 1934, and totaled at least 8 percent for the rest of the decade.

The New Deal gave way to World War II (or, in Roosevelt's words, "Dr. New Deal" gave way to "Dr. Win the War"). The United States led the Allies to victory and assumed the role of global leader. It also raised tax rates to the approximate average level they have been ever since. The nation, which had experienced an expansive growth of domestic government and the emergence of a new national security state, would not look back. Government begat more government as Americans increasingly sought help from Washington.

As government assumed more functions, policymakers created more departments to perform them: Health and Human Services in 1953, Housing and Urban Development in 1965, Transportation in 1966, Energy in 1967, Education in 1979, Veterans Affairs in 1987, and Homeland Security in 2002. Thus, policymakers have nearly doubled the president's Cabinet since the New Deal, with each of those new departments running new programs that, together, drove up total government domestic spending significantly as tax levels were maintained and defense levels fell.[19]

Beyond the Cabinet, policymakers created a host of other agencies, including the Securities and Exchange Commission, Federal Deposit Insurance Corporation, Fish and Wildlife Service, Federal Aviation Administration, Federal Highway Administration, Consumer Product Safety Commission, Environmental Protection Agency, Nuclear Regulatory Commission, International Trade Administration, and many others. Some agencies of relatively recent vintage, such as the Environmental Protection Agency, have enjoyed unofficial Cabinet status under recent presidents.[20]

Cabinet departments created new senior positions and filled them with increasing numbers of slots (for example, moving from one deputy to two or from two assistant secretaries to four). Presidential appointees who required Senate confirmation grew exponentially, from 71 in 1933 to an estimated 1,217 in 2012.[21] Roosevelt created the Executive Office of the President in 1939 and, today, it has a staff of over 1,800 full-time equivalents.[22] Similar growth occurred with congressional committees and their staffs.[23]

In the post-World War II era, both parties and every president built on the foundation that Roosevelt had set, cumulatively creating a slew of new federal programs and activities. Recession and war, retirement and health care, education and jobs, food safety and environmental protection—each party looks to the federal government to define and address problems.

Meanwhile, more private interests (big and small businesses, colleges and teachers, farmers and food companies, homebuilders and mortgage brokers) set up shop in Washington in the form of trade associations and interest groups to protect the largesse that government was providing to their members. Business, labor, foundations, and well-heeled individuals of the right and left established think tanks, policy shops, and other entities to pursue their policy goals. When any of these organizations could not achieve their goals on their own, they hired from among the growing legion of lobbyists.

To a great extent, power in Washington derives from the size of the budget over which one presides or the legislation that one can influence. On any issue, an executive department, congressional committee, or private group has every incentive to expand its favored programs. If it cannot get a spending increase, a tax break often will do. On issue after issue, the three sectors (executive, congressional, and private) work together in what political scientists call "iron triangles."[24]

In this activist world, politics and economics mix in interesting ways, with the parties often mirroring one another. Over the years, Republicans were as responsible for increases in Social Security benefits as Democrats, while it was President George W. Bush and a Republican-controlled Congress that enacted the last major Medicare expansion in 2003, providing drug coverage to senior citizens. Democrats from President Kennedy onward often spearheaded tax cuts to improve the economy and backed them as often as Republicans, even though Keynes had initially argued that spending increases provide more bang-for-the-buck stimulus. Republicans came to revere the Kennedy tax cuts, arguing that they proved the supply side value of tax cutting.

Both parties allotted tax cuts to the large middle class, even though supply-side doctrine focuses on the top tax rate that high-income groups pay and Keynesianism implies that concentrating money on lower-income groups would better stimulate demand because they would more likely spend the money. Both the Reagan and George W. Bush tax cuts included tax cuts at all income levels and raised personal exemptions and child credits. Obama championed a cut in Social Security taxes that was available to almost all workers, not just those with low or moderate incomes.

Both parties provided more tax subsidies and allowed permanent ones to grow significantly, moving the code further from its basic function, which is to raise revenue. From the tax exclusion for employer-provided health care to the home mortgage deduction to write-offs for

IRAs and 401(k) plans, tax breaks drained federal revenues. While subsidies hidden in the tax code at first seem to reduce the size of government by reducing its net revenue claim, in fact they do the opposite. They interfere ever more in the economy by subsidizing certain activities over others and adding to the interest costs and debt burdens of future generations.

In effect, aside from debates over whether to raise taxes on those at the very top or cut spending for those at the bottom, Democrats and Republicans often came to the same policy conclusions. They curried favor with middle-class voters by showering them with additional giveaways, adding provision after provision with little concern for fundamental principles of simplicity or equal justice. They exploited the economic doctrines of Keynesianism or supply side theory, invoked them to justify almost any spending or tax giveaway, and fought at best over whose giveaway was better.

4

Postwar Fiscal Policy:
The Gradual Demise
of Fiscal Democracy

*"Prisoner, tell me, who was it that wrought this
unbreakable chain?"*

*"It was I," said the prisoner, "who forged this
chain very carefully. I thought my invincible power
would hold the world captive leaving me in a freedom undisturbed. Thus night and day I worked at the
chain with huge fires and cruel hard strokes. When at
last the work was done and the links were complete
and unbreakable, I found that it held me in its grip."*

—Rabindranath Tagore, Gitanjali

Fiscal policy moves in no straight line. It ebbs and flows,
responding to economic or fiscal conditions, emerging needs, or other
challenges. The period since World War II is no exception.

We have already examined some of the forces that moved us toward
our current state. Economic policy in the twentieth century increasingly
opened the door to more deficit spending, as tax cuts delivered both
Keynesian stimulus or supply side incentives and domestic spending
expanding government's size and scope as it responded to a greater
number of social and economic needs. Democratic and Republican policymakers alike not only promised to deliver more good things if elected,
but trusted the federal government to solve a growing array of economic
and social problems, whether through higher benefits or lower taxes.

Elected officials also created an array of permanent programs,
expanded their average benefits and roster of eligible recipients, and
then enabled some of the largest programs to grow automatically faster

than the economy—no matter what other needs emerged along the way. Those mandatory or entitlement programs then increasingly came to dominate the budget. Together, these forces combined to produce the sharp fall in our fiscal freedom.

Since World War II, however, the trend toward declining fiscal freedom has moved less along a linear path than a downward spiral. In broad terms, we can identify three distinct legislative eras that have brought us to our current fiscal turning point. They are distinguished from one another largely by the dominance of either "giveaways" or "takeaways."[1] At times, policymakers found themselves flush with public cash and only too eager to capitalize on it by creating a host of new programs and tax cuts. At other times, they fretted over the rise in deficits and worked to rein in the red ink.

Let us take a closer look at each of these eras and see how the legislative habits that were nourished within them play out today.

The Era of Easy Finance: 1945–1981

In the aftermath of World War II, policymakers enacted a huge number of legislative initiatives to boost domestic spending—on Social Security, Medicare, Medicaid, education, housing, highways, and much more. Meanwhile, tax cuts grew increasingly common, with elected officials and their constituents expecting one almost every year by the end of this era.

How could the numbers add up? How could policymakers give away more and more in the form of higher spending and lower taxes and still balance the federal books (or remain within striking distance of doing so)? Mostly, it was *not* because policymakers enacted compensating tax increases and spending cuts. In fact, on the relatively few occasions in which they raised taxes or cut spending, it usually came in the context of broader legislation that focused on giveaways. For instance, policymakers linked Social Security tax hikes with Social Security benefit increases of even greater long-term cost, and the one modest income tax surcharge of 1968–69 at the peak of the Vietnam War came as part of a long-run package of tax cuts.[2]

Instead, the answer to our riddle lies elsewhere. Federal revenues grew rapidly and automatically as the economy grew robustly during this period. In addition, revenues grew even faster than rising incomes as inflation and real increases in incomes pushed more Americans into higher tax brackets (a process known as "bracket creep"). Only in this postwar period had inflation become a more permanent feature of the economy.

Next, defense policy set the stage for increased domestic spending in two ways. First, all of the large twentieth-century tax increases derived from wartime policy when policymakers raised taxes to finance the nation's military action.[3] When the wars ended, policymakers might cut taxes a bit but, especially after World War II and the Korean Conflict, they largely kept higher tax levels in place, enabling them to expand the size and scope of government during peacetime. Since World War II, tax levels have largely remained constant, when measured as a percent of national income.

Second, despite major U.S. engagements in Korea and Vietnam that boosted defense spending episodically, defense spending generally fell over this period as a share of the budget and the economy. Consequently, policymakers could shift huge sums of former defense dollars to the domestic side by transferring so-called "peace dividends." In the first few years after the Korean Conflict, over half of all federal taxes went to finance defense. As defense spending fell, an ever-larger share of those tax dollars went to finance domestic spending.

Since the end of World War II, defense spending has tended to follow a boom and bust pattern, with defense "build-ups" followed by "build-downs" when wars ended, threats subsided, or both. Not surprisingly, the build-downs came in the aftermaths of World War II, Korea, Vietnam, and the Cold War. The largest build-downs tended to provide the greatest source of newly available funds to fuel domestic expansions. Though Republicans are often closely associated in the public mind with robust defense spending, Republican presidents have tended to preside during these periods of defense build-downs and domestic expansions. Republicans of this vintage included Dwight Eisenhower in the 1950s (post-Korea), Richard Nixon in 1969 and the early 1970s (post-Vietnam), and George H. W. Bush (post-Cold War). (See Appendix.)

Compare, for instance, defense spending at the end of the Korean Conflict (14 percent of GDP in 1953) with defense spending at the height of the Iraq and Afghanistan wars (5 percent of GDP in 2010 and 2011, and even lower today). This decline essentially enabled a shift of nine percentage points of GDP a year to domestic spending without a tax increase. At today's level of GDP, those nine percentage points total about $1.5 trillion a year. Most of that shift had occurred by 1981. The next three decades then brought two more cycles of build-ups and build-downs (the Reagan-era build-up and post-Cold War build-down, followed by a post–September 11 build-up and troop withdrawal from Iraq and Afghanistan).

In addition, inflation tended to rise in stages during this easy finance period, so that real interest rates were often low and even negative. Bondholders willing to accept a 4 percent return when inflation was 2 percent might find later on that inflation had risen also to 4 percent and their returns were effectively zero. That limited the real interest payments that the federal government was required to make on the federal debt. While the nation emerged from World War II with the highest level of public debt (as a share of GDP) in its history, the interest rates that it was paying on that debt were relatively low. Factoring in inflation, they were often negative.

Consequently, the debt-to-GDP ratio fell dramatically in the post-World War II Era of Easy Finance, despite moderate deficits—all while policymakers were enacting more domestic legislation and cutting taxes. Hypothetically, an economy with a debt of 70 percent of GDP and a nominal GDP growth (real plus inflationary) rate of 6 percent can bear deficits of 4.2 percent of GDP without its debt-to-GDP ratio rising.

Social Security and Medicare tax increases provided one major exception to the general trend toward lower taxes. But, politically speaking, that is a bit misleading. Tax increases for Social Security did not make waves partly because only the young and future generations would have to pay the higher rates over a lifetime to finance benefit increases for older generations who either paid no tax for years or paid at a lower rate during part or much of their working lives.[4] In effect, voters always got back more than they put in because many costs were passed onto the young, who were not yet voting.[5] Even as late as 1980—forty-five years after Social Security was first enacted—a two-earner couple making the average wage who retired at age 65 would have paid $219,000 of Social Security and Medicare taxes over their lifetime, but would receive $635,000 worth of benefits.[6]

In essence, policymakers of this period enjoyed an enormous degree of fiscal freedom. When it came to legislation, they could focus almost entirely on giveaways, especially with respect to domestic policy.

But the Era of Easy Finance was followed by an Era of Fiscal Straight-jackets, starting in 1982 (and to which we will turn in the next section). Historical eras, however, do not tend to start and end abruptly. The seeds of a later era are often planted in the latter stages of an earlier one. The transition from the Era of Easy Finance to the Era of Fiscal Straightjackets was no exception. The seeds of the latter were planted in a turbulent last period of the former, from about 1973 to 1981.

It was not an easy time in America, and new challenges influenced the budget conversation. Vietnam had opened deep (and still agoniz-ing) public divisions over America's place in the world. Watergate con-firmed Americans' worst suspicions about their leaders and nourished a cynicism about politics that only grew in the decades that followed. The economy did little to brighten spirits, as the strong economic growth and rising living standards that had largely characterized the post-World War II period came to an end. Inflation continued to accelerate, spurred by oil price shocks. Stagflation—a stagnating but inflating economy—came to define the transition period. Meanwhile, entitlement spending grew rapidly, increasingly came to dominate federal spending, and con-sequently left elected officials with less ability to enact new policies in the ways to which they had become accustomed.

Turmoil ensued between and within the two parties. After Watergate and Nixon's resignation, Republicans were a spent and divided force. While Democrats benefited from Republican disarray, electing a huge number of new lawmakers in the 1974 mid-term elections and regaining the White House with Jimmy Carter in 1976, they often fought among themselves. Many Democratic lawmakers wanted to continue spend-ing as they had in the earlier part of the Era of Easy Finance, and they expressed little support for Carter's efforts at fiscal rectitude, such as his idea of basing spending choices on cost-benefit analysis. Besides, Carter had run for president as a Washington "outsider" and, once in office, he embraced the image in his relations with Congress, fueling further conflict between the branches.

By the late 1970s, signs of the fiscal straightjackets yet to come began to appear. In 1977, Congress enacted the first-ever major cuts in Social Security through a paring of a very high, and accidental, rate of benefit growth that derived from technical errors in a 1973 law.[7] Nevertheless, Congress retained a modified version of the 1973 provision that called for annual, automatic increases in benefits. That decision has ensured that, to this day, annual benefits grow from one generation to the next one at the rate of growth in average wages. And that—along with an automatic growth in benefits as life expectancy expanded and the then forthcoming decline in workers-per-retiree due to a fall in the birth rate—effectively left Social Security growing faster than the economy indefinitely and descending into permanent long-term imbalance.

Although Congress cut taxes almost annually in the high inflation period of the late 1970s, the tax cuts did not keep many Americans from facing higher income tax rates due to bracket creep. Some upper-middle income families saw their marginal tax rate (the tax rate they paid on the last dollar earned) double from near 22 percent to over 40 percent.[8] Even lower-income Americans were affected, as the value of personal and dependent exemptions and the effective tax-exempt level of income eroded, pulling even the poor into paying income taxes and leading to a broader base on which income taxes were applied. Moreover, inflation and taxes interacted in ways that caused real estate values to rapidly rise, as the cost of mortgage borrowing often ended up negative after taking taxes into account. Higher real estate values, in turn, led to continually higher property taxes.

Facing higher taxes, Americans launched tax revolts at the ballot boxes. The most famous revolt against rising property taxes was California's Proposition 13, which generally held rates of property tax increases well below rates of economic growth for existing, but not necessarily new, homeowners.[9]

Sluggish growth, rising inflation and taxes, and tax revolts all nourished a political environment on which another Washington "outsider," Ronald Reagan, could capitalize. He campaigned for president on a platform of cutting taxes, boosting defense spending, and cutting waste from domestic spending. That was no new stance for the former actor. When he was inaugurated as California's governor in 1967, he declared, "We stand between the taxpayer and the taxspender."[10]

As soon as Reagan won the Republican presidential nomination in 1980, his campaign staff began to analyze and draft tax legislation. Mid-way through 1981, after months of effort to gather the requisite votes in Congress, Reagan signed the Economic Recovery Tax Act, providing a 23 percent tax cut for individuals, business tax breaks that would expand an already growing array of tax shelters, and tax brackets "indexed" so that inflation would no longer push taxpayers into higher tax brackets. When Reagan's economic advisors warned him about his plan's potential for rising deficits, he replied, "I don't care."[11]

Reagan's fiscal policy symbolized a movement that had been underway for years in conservative circles to restrain the size of government. In that sense, it is tempting to locate early Reaganism in the next era— that of fiscal straightjackets. Nevertheless, the 1981 tax cuts represents the last major thrust of the Era of Easy Financing—the last of the large domestic giveaways that policymakers did not finance up front through offsetting tax increases or spending cuts. From a Republican perspective, it was now their turn to give away money—but in their own way. Unlike earlier conservatives who questioned government's power to remake society, these new-era conservative activists argued that a drop in tax burdens of a couple of percentage points of GDP could dramatically boost economic growth.

The 1981 tax cut presaged, and indeed catalyzed, movement into the era that was to come next. In contrast to earlier giveaways that characterized this easy financing period, the tax cut could not be financed by other automatic sources of funds (for example, bracket creep, lower defense spending, and a relative decline in domestic programs that had little built-in automatic annual growth).

By themselves, the tax cuts do not tell the full story of why deficits and debt were both rising as this era came to a close. Receipts never fell below 17.3 percent of GDP under Reagan (a level reached in 1984), and that 17.3 percent figure is not much lower than the 18.0 percent level of the early part of Carter's presidency (1977 and 1978). Moreover, revenues rose as a share of GDP later in Reagan's term (for example, 18.4 percent in 1987 and 18.2 percent in 1988) because the economy grew stronger and because Reagan and Congress raised taxes numerous times to ensure that the deficits of those years, though large, did not grow even larger.

Deficits and rising debt-to-GDP ratios after 1981, therefore, derived from a combination of factors that stretched well beyond the tax cuts and even Reagan's defense build-up.

The Era of Fiscal Straightjackets: 1982–1997

As the Era of Fiscal Straightjackets arrived, all sources of easy finance from the previous era had begun to dry up.

Take economic growth. Although, for much of the 1980s and 1990s, the economy grew faster than in the mid-to-late 1970s, it never returned on a long-term basis to its post-World War II highs. Such highs nourished an unrealistic expectation, because they came at a time when the United States dominated the world economy, with Europe and Asia recovering from the wreckage of World War II. Meanwhile, a deep recession in the early 1980s added further to the deficits that the 1981 tax cuts and defense build-up had fueled.

Or, take inflation. Inflation fell due to the efforts of Federal Reserve Board Chairman Paul Volcker, who assumed his post in 1979 with a fierce determination to wring inflation from the economy. (Volcker, whose monetary tightening initially sent the economy reeling and unemployment soaring, says that he told President Carter that if the latter appointed him, his policies would likely make Carter a one-term president.[12]) The lower inflation that Volcker helped to produce had two major consequences for our fiscal story. First, lower inflation would no longer reduce the value of federal debt as much as higher inflation had been doing. And second, lower inflation generated lower revenues due to less bracket creep from 1981 to 1984—before the brackets were indexed to inflation.

Or, take defense. Defense's share of the budget climbed as Reagan pushed large spending increases through Congress through his first term—though it would begin to fall again as a percent of GDP by the end of his second term and during the tenure of his successor, George H. W. Bush. In fact, it was Carter who initiated the defense spending increases on which Reagan would build.

Perhaps most importantly, entitlement spending continued to rise as a share of the budget. With high built-in growth rates, programs including Social Security, Medicare, and Medicaid would absorb an ever-larger portion of any new revenues available to government, put ever-larger pressure on the budget as a whole, and force policymakers to cut elsewhere or accept the reality of larger deficits.

Consequently, as this era took shape, budget experts routinely predicted a future of budget deficits "as far as the eye can see."[13] In Washington, fears of what such persistent deficits could produce (soaring inflation, skyrocketing interest rates, perhaps even economic collapse) prompted policymakers to shift course dramatically, moving from giveaways to takeaways. Presidents Reagan, George H. W. Bush, and Bill

Clinton worked with Congress in their tenures to enact major deficit reduction agreements in 1982, 1984, 1990, and 1993, and modest ones in other years. Partly because of the stalemate between the two political parties, they enacted no significant tax cuts until 1997 (although they cut some taxes in the context of raising others during this period), they stabilized discretionary spending in real terms and cut it as a share of GDP, and they enacted no major entitlement expansions, while converting one welfare entitlement, Aid to Families with Dependent Children (AFDC), into a non-entitlement program, Temporary Assistance for Needy Families (TANF).

Moreover, in reforming Social Security in 1983 to strengthen the program financially, they enacted a number of significant tax increases, such as by subjecting some Social Security benefits to income tax. They also pared the rate of growth in benefits, particularly through the first-ever increase in the "normal" retirement age (the age at which "full" benefits are available) for a population whose life expectancy continued to rise.

By beginning to address some of these fiscal challenges—reducing deficits in 1982 and 1984 and reforming Social Security in 1983—policymakers gave themselves some running room to overhaul the income tax code in 1986. The landmark Tax Reform Act of 1986 was the product of years of groundwork in the Treasury Department and on Capitol Hill.

Reagan's Treasury Department unveiled a comprehensive proposal in 1984 (full disclosure: I served as original organizer and economic coordinator of that effort), while key lawmakers had issued their own proposals in the early 1980s, the most original and complete of which was by Senator Bill Bradley (D-NJ) and Congressman Richard Gephardt (D-MO). The 1986 act represented the most fundamental base-broadening reform of the income tax since its inception over seventy years earlier, eliminating hundreds of billions of dollars of tax deductions, credits, and other tax write-offs in exchange for lower tax rates, higher exemptions, and better tax treatment of the poor and families with children.

Once again, policymakers imposed substantial takeaways—this time to finance lower rates. The law cut rates for middle- and higher-income Americans and freed millions of low-income families from paying income taxes at all by raising tax thresholds and expanding benefits for low-income families such as the Earned Income Tax Credit (EITC). But, to finance the rate cuts, the law expanded the tax base, particularly for higher-income groups (and a bit for lower income groups as well) while scaling back tax shelters.[14]

The effort was a thoroughly bipartisan affair. In Reagan's Treasury Department, Secretaries Donald Regan and then James Baker led the effort while fighting opposition from within the administration, such as from other departments that were trying to protect their constituencies (for example, the Energy Department seeking to protect write-offs for oil and gas drilling).

On Capitol Hill, Senate Republicans Howard Baker (the majority leader through 1984), Robert Dole (the Finance Committee chairman and then, starting in 1985, the majority leader), and Bob Packwood (the Finance Committee chairman after Dole) worked with such key Senate Democrats as Finance Committee members Bill Bradley and George Mitchell. In the House, Ways and Means Committee chairman Dan Rostenkowski, a wily pol from Chicago, led the effort. Reagan and Rostenkowski agreed to work together, maintain close relations, and limit criticisms of one another's ideas publicly, especially when Rostenkowski was trying to push a bill through his committee.

Far more important to the nation's fiscal future, however, were the budget agreements that policymakers enacted in 1990 and 1993—the first a bipartisan agreement under President George H. W. Bush, the second a Democrat-only agreement under President Clinton. They were both highly controversial and, unlike the deficit-cutting agreements under Reagan, they both came to impose considerable political costs on the presidents who spearheaded them.

With the 1990 agreement, Bush violated his famous "read my lips, no new taxes" pledge that he enunciated in his acceptance speech at the 1988 Republican National Convention. Although the tax increases of that deal were modest, they became a cause célèbre among more ideological Republicans, many of whom had never trusted Bush to begin with and now considered him a traitor to their cause. Outraged by the tax increases, House Republican whip Newt Gingrich led a GOP revolt that defeated the first agreement between Bush and congressional negotiators. White House and congressional negotiators were forced to return to the bargaining table to craft a second deal, which they pushed through Congress.

Notwithstanding the controversy surrounding it, the 1990 Budget Enforcement Act was one of the largest and most successful acts of the deficit-cutting era, making a number of fundamental changes in budget policy that constrained spending increases and tax cuts for a decade (see below). Nevertheless, Bush's no-tax flip, along with a recession in 1991 that was still on the minds of voters in 1992, surely contributed significantly to Bush's re-election defeat.

When Bill Clinton assumed the presidency in 1993, he had plenty of reasons to focus on deficit reduction. For one thing, despite Bush's efforts, deficits were projected to rise through the 1990s and beyond. For another, Clinton had pledged to cut the deficit in half by the end of his first term. For still another, congressional Democrats had continually fought against the deficits that they attributed to Reagan and, in particular, his tax cuts in 1981. With a Democrat now in the White House, it was put-up-or-shut-up time for the Democratic Party. Finally, Ross Perot had run for president in 1992 and garnered 19 percent of the vote as a third-party candidate focused on the deficit, and Clinton did not want that 19 percent of voters to question his deficit-cutting bona fides. Thus, not surprisingly, Clinton sided with the deficit "hawks" among his economic advisers, who urged him to focus early on deficit-cutting, as opposed to the political operatives who urged him first to fulfill his campaign pledge to cut taxes for middle-income Americans.

Clinton cut the deficit but, as with Bush, it came with a serious political cost. In the agreement that he crafted solely with congressional Democrats—every Republican lawmaker voted against it—Clinton agreed to raise income taxes for the wealthiest Americans while boosting the federal tax on gasoline. That is, not only did Clinton *not* cut taxes for the middle class as he had promised, he raised them, however moderately, for everyone who drove.

This backpedalling, along with some other early failures, was too much for the voters a year later. In the 1994 congressional elections, voters gave control of both houses of Congress to Republicans for the first time since the early 1950s. Not a single Republican incumbent in Congress lost that year. But lots of Democrats did, including House Speaker Tom Foley (D-WA).

To be sure, while Bush suffered from the weak economy of 1992, Clinton suffered in 1994 from the debacle of his health reform effort, opposition to gun control legislation that he pushed through Congress, early controversies over gays in the military, and a general sense of disarray within his administration. Nevertheless, each man also suffered due to his willingness to take away something from the public by raising taxes—whatever the gains for deficit reduction.

Politicians have long memories. They learn from the experiences of their predecessors, positive and negative. After the 1992 and 1994 elections, the legend took hold that the road to political ruin runs through tax increases. A similar legend had long held on the spending side, where Social Security was considered the "third rail" of American politics—touch it and you die. More generally, elected officials were squeamish about asking anybody to give up anything—to pay higher taxes or receive fewer benefits—in the interest of fiscal sanity.

The 1993 budget deal was the last significant legislative action to reduce deficits until some fledgling efforts beginning in 2011 that led to spending cuts in 2013 and beyond. That long lull was due in part to the budget politics described above as well as to the state of fiscal affairs. Through the rest of the 1990s, deficits fell from year to year until they disappeared in 1998, when Washington ran its first surplus since 1969 and followed with three more from 1999 to 2001. Not surprisingly, Clinton and congressional Democrats claimed full credit for the fiscal turnaround but, as always, history was a bit more complex.

To be sure, the 1993 agreement was important. But, its savings represented a smaller a share of the economy than the 1990 agreement; both claimed $500 billion in savings over five years but, due to inflation, a dollar was worth more in 1990 than 1993. Larger than either of those deals, however, was the 1982 agreement between Reagan and Congress.[15]

More important than just the savings, the 1990 and 1993 agreements created a set of processes that limited discretionary spending and imposed hurdles on new entitlements and tax cuts. Together, these processes protected the deficit reductions of 1990 and 1993 by holding spending and tax cuts largely in check while the economy grew and a confluence of other factors raised revenues and held the entitlement juggernaut briefly at bay.

Specifically, on the discretionary side, the agreements imposed a set of annual "caps" on total discretionary spending, which essentially held that spending category constant (in real terms) in upcoming years. Rather than force the public to swallow "cuts" in discretionary programs, Congress achieved savings by not letting such spending rise in real terms even as the economy grew. These agreements also imposed a "pay-as-you-go" (PAYGO) requirement on entitlements and tax cuts.

Policymakers could not enact legislation to create or expand an entitlement or cut a tax without offsetting the costs by cutting other entitlements or raising other taxes.

Adding to the fiscal constraints was a stalemate between Democratic Clinton and a Republican Congress that essentially checked both sides from allocating significant giveaways (although the parties reformed welfare, immigration, telecommunications, and other policies and expanded trade). Indeed, by the end of his two terms, Clinton presided over domestic spending declines as a share of the economy that were similar to those under Reagan and that rank him near the bottom of modern-day domestic spending presidents (see Appendix).

In the late 1990s, the two parties even fought over which could more ably create government surpluses by balancing the non-Social Security part of the budget while Social Security was running a modest surplus (due to the huge numbers of baby boomers who were in the work force and, in turn, paying payroll taxes to support the program). That marked a change from the nation's traditional fiscal policy, in which the government typically ran even larger deficits outside of Social Security while the program accumulated surpluses.

Meanwhile, Bush and Clinton (and Congress during their tenures) benefited from the peace dividend that came with the fall of the Berlin Wall, the crack-up of the Soviet empire, and the end of the Cold War. Once again, policymakers could shift dollars that previously went for defense to help them finance domestic programs, cut deficits, or both.

Clinton also benefited from a few peculiarities of his time. One was a long period of economic growth without recession, producing what his aides called a "virtuous cycle" of lower deficits and interest rates, more savings and investment, and more growth and jobs. Each element of this cycle fed upon the others so that lower deficits led to more savings, lower interest rates led to more investment, and more savings and investment led to more growth and jobs.

A second peculiarity was an asset bubble market, especially in tech stock. The tech stock bubble, which sent the NASDAQ to levels far exceeding the underlying values of the companies in question, enabled many upper-income people to exercise their stock options or sell their stocks and realize gains on which they would then pay capital gains tax. Income tax revenues flourished. (A second asset bubble was to come before the Great Recession of 2007–08.)

A third peculiarity came in a key area of federal spending. Spending on health care entitlements slowed during the last few years of the twentieth century, largely due to the creation of health maintenance organizations (HMOs) and preferred provider organizations (PPOs). After this brief delay, however, health care spending resumed its relentless rise.

Finally, both health and retirement spending were held in check a bit by a low birth-rate population of Depression and World War II babies retiring, while the baby boomers reached their peak earning and taxpaying years.

By 1997, the Era of Fiscal Straightjackets had run its course. That year, Clinton and Congress enacted a bipartisan deficit reduction agreement, which was designed to bring the deficit problem of the 1980s and early 1990s to an end. The 1997 agreement may have been intended to put a firm final stamp on austerity, but the ensuing surpluses planted the seeds of the profligacy that returned in later years.

In that 1997 agreement, Clinton and Congress enacted a series of health care cost containment measures that they later largely rescinded. Also, they enacted a series of modest tax cuts, helping fulfill both a traditional Republican push for lower taxes as well as Clinton's 1992 campaign pledge to cut taxes for middle-income Americans. Those actions call into question whether the 1997 agreement over time even reduced deficits. Regardless, as budget surpluses began to accumulate, policymakers engaged in a new debate—what to do with the money. As the twentieth century gave way to the twenty-first, lawmakers had tasted the fruits of tax cutting. They soon wanted more.

The Era of Two Santas: 1997–2010

In early March of 1976, long-time *Wall Street Journal* editorial writer Jude Wanniski penned a piece for the *National Observer,* "Taxes and a Two-Santa Theory."[16] It was one of those rare pieces of writing that would foretaste a change in the course of history, as Republicans transformed themselves from a party that traditionally imposed fiscal pain to an activist one that offered fiscal pleasure.

"Simply stated," Wanniski wrote for the now-defunct publication, "the Two Santa Claus Theory is this: For the U.S. economy to be healthy and grow, there must be a division of labor between Democrats and Republicans; each must be a different kind of Santa Claus." Wanniski continued:

The Democrats, the party of income redistribution, are best suited for the role of Spending Santa Claus. The Republicans, traditionally the party of income growth, should be the Santa Claus of Tax Reduction. It has been the failure of the GOP to stick to this traditional role that has caused much of the nation's economic misery. Only the shrewdness of the Democrats, who have kindly agreed to play both Santa Clauses during critical periods, has saved the nation from even greater misery.

It isn't that Republicans don't enjoy cutting taxes. They love it. But there is something in the Republican chemistry that causes the GOP to become hypnotized by the prospect of an imbalanced budget. Static analysis tells them taxes can't be cut or inflation will result. They either argue for a tax hike to dampen inflation when the economy is in a boom or demand spending cuts to balance the budget when the economy is in recession.

In essence, Wanniski argued that Republicans should return to their tax-cutting roots in the 1920s, to the era of Republican Presidents Warren Harding, Calvin Coolidge, and Herbert Hoover, each of them served by Treasury Secretary Andrew Mellon. Back then, Republicans cut taxes at least five times (though this was largely a pull-back from wartime tax rates). Perhaps more important for the supply-side fiscal policy that would come decades later, Mellon argued that tax cuts would provide such a boost in economic activity that the government would reap greater revenues than if policymakers had not cut taxes to begin with.

The point was not just fiscal; it was also political. As Democrats hand out goodies on the spending side, they curried favor from the voters. As Republicans imposed pain by focusing on budget balancing, they lost support from voters. The way for Republicans to boost the economy, raise revenues, and compete better with Democrats, Wanniski said, was to cut taxes.

Wanniski summed up the situation for Republicans this way:

They embrace the role of Scrooge, playing into the hands of the Democrats, who know the first rule of successful politics is Never Shoot Santa Claus. The political tension in the market place of ideas must be between tax reduction and spending increases, and as long as Republicans have insisted on balanced budgets, their influence as a party has shriveled, and budgets have been imbalanced.

Thus, Democrats had long focused on allotting giveaways. Wanniski argued that Republicans should do the same.

Fine. But, an all-giveaway competition creates an obvious problem. The budget is basically a balance sheet. Every dollar that is spent must be paid by someone, at some point.[17] Put another way, spending today equals taxes that are paid today, plus taxes that are deferred to the future—just as household spending today equals bills that a household pays today and the bills that it defers to the future. In both cases, deferred bill-paying also adds to future spending in the form of higher interest payments on additional borrowing.

Like Mellon in the 1920s and supply-siders like Arthur Laffer in the 1970s, Wanniski argued that tax cuts would pay for themselves. So, too, did the editorial page for which he worked. Tax cuts would stimulate the economy enough to eventually solve the fiscal problem.

Wanniski seemed to assume that Republican Santa Claus-ism would compete with its Democratic counterpart. The former would push for tax cuts, the latter for spending increases. When the former won, government would shrink as the private sector grew.

What would happen, however, if the parties competed with one another over who could be the Santa with the biggest bag of goodies? What if policymakers enacted ever-more tax cuts and spending increases? What if the two Santas appeared together, rather than one at a time? Wanniski never confronted the possibility or, if he did, he never seemed troubled by it. But, that's what happened under President George W. Bush after the turn of the century as policy makers cut taxes, boosted defense and domestic discretionary spending, and expanded entitlements mainly by adding prescription drug coverage to Medicare.

Bush was no piker on either the tax or spending side. No president in U.S. history engaged in so much tax cutting along with faster spending in every category as a share of GDP. Reagan cut domestic discretionary spending as a share of the budget; Roosevelt in the end cut domestic spending as a share of GDP even below the levels that he inherited from Hoover; and Nixon largely offset his dramatic domestic expansion with large cuts in defense. Even Lyndon Johnson, who is best known for boosting both defense and domestic spending ("guns and butter"), presided over significant tax increases mainly from bracket creep and backed a surtax as his administration was ending.

As Bush campaigned for president in 2000, the budget was in the black, accumulating surpluses that were beginning to significantly reduce the nation's outstanding debt. The White House Office of Management and Budget, Congressional Budget Office, and private budget experts all predicted that surpluses would grow for the near-term future, with lower interest costs to some extent offsetting ever rising health and retirement costs. Policymakers even pondered the possibility that surpluses would temporarily pay off the entire debt, raising the question of what the government would then do with the surplus dollars that would accumulate after that.

Bush had pledged to cut taxes enough to give Americans $1 back for every $4 of expected surpluses. "It's not the government's money," he told voters during his contest with Vice President Al Gore. "It's your money." It all sounded reasonable. Gore promised to cut taxes as well. But, while Bush pledged to cut tax rates across the board, Gore proposed targeted tax cuts to spur activity in what he considered socially worthwhile ventures.

Once in office, Bush's fiscal expansions were impressive. Working with a Republican-controlled Congress through 2006:

- Bush cut taxes for individuals in 2001, small businesses in 2002, individuals again in 2003, and corporations in 2004. Among other things, he cut individual income tax rates, greatly eased the tax on estates, cut taxes on capital gains and dividends, and cut taxes for domestic manufacturers.
- Bush had promised to increase defense spending, and that campaign pledge became a no-brainer after the terrorist attacks of September 11. While boosting the underlying defense budget, Bush also took the nation to war in Afghanistan and Iraq, further boosting defense spending over its levels in the peaceful days of the late 1990s.
- Unwilling to veto legislation that emerged from a Republican-controlled Congress and, more broadly, unwilling to confront members of his party over spending, he let domestic discretionary spending grow as well.
- With an eye on his 2004 reelection and the all-important vote of senior citizens, Bush added prescription drug coverage for the elderly to Medicare. The 2003 legislation that included this expansion marked the first major entitlement increase in the nation's

history with no significant revenue source to finance it. It also marked a major expansion of a federal program that was already projected to be increasingly out of balance.

The growth in entitlements was already absorbing large portions of any revenues that economic growth would generate. The nation also was a far cry from the Era of Easy Finance and its many automatic sources of funds to finance an expansion of domestic spending or more tax cuts (for example, peace dividends and inflationary income tax bracket creep were no longer available).

Cognizant of entitlement growth, Bush tried to reform Social Security—twice, in fact. First, he appointed a commission under Daniel Patrick Moynihan, former Democratic Senator from New York, who played a major behind-the-scenes role in the 1983 Social Security reform. Then, he promised to "spend his capital" in his second term partly to reform Social Security. He complicated matters greatly, however, by trying to allocate some Social Security taxes to fund private accounts, run much larger budget deficits for decades as a result, and later gradually recapture the losses through future benefit cuts.

Democrats were in no mood to compromise with Bush after the bitterly contested presidential election in 2000 and controversial aftermath, and they attacked the effort to "privatize" Social Security. The problem went beyond politics, however. Even with a better designed and more politically tenable plan, the government lacked the resources to finance it in ways that would offend few households. By now, policy makers lacked the fiscal freedom to finance deficit increases that might accompany a transition to a different system. Moreover, elected officials had not sought to impose a significant takeaway on the public for more than a decade, and they were not ready to do so now. Bush asked the public to pay for almost nothing, and the Democrats were in no hurry to do otherwise.

The Bush presidency was followed by that of Barack Obama, elected in the midst of an economic crisis that was fueled by a financial collapse and a deepening recession, each feeding on the other to create the greatest economic challenge since the Great Depression.

Like all new presidents, Obama promised to shift course, to turn sharply away from the failed policies of the past, to put his own stamp on the size, scope, and direction of government. In reality, he continued the general thrust of his predecessor's fiscal policy. Policymakers still focused mainly on giveaways, even if an all-Democratic government now favored spending giveaways rather than tax giveaways. Bush had had his turn; many Democrats now felt it was theirs.

Their efforts largely fell into two categories. First, with tens of millions of Americans still without health insurance, Obama and congressional Democrats sought to address one of the nation's real sore points and fulfill the party's longstanding hopes of extending universal health coverage to all Americans—a hope that dated back to President Harry S. Truman.

Second, the recession demanded a response, and the limits of monetary policy to push interest rates below zero rejuvenated the power of Keynesian thinking in addressing the most severe decline in consumer demand since the Great Depression. At the same time, it was hard to decipher whether the tax cuts and spending increases that policymakers pursued were supposed to be temporary or permanent. Thus, Obama proposed a permanent extension of the Bush's tax cuts, which were due to expire at the end of 2010, for all but the most well-to-do Americans, along with other tax cuts and spending increases to fight the recession.

With regard to the rising longer-term deficits that he inherited (and to which he added with his efforts to rejuvenate the economy), Obama expressed only limited interest, investing some hope in portions of comprehensive health reform, which Congress enacted in 2010 in what's known as the Affordable Care Act. Obama's aides noted that rising health care costs represented the greatest long-term obstacle to reducing projected deficits but de-emphasized the growing impact of demographic forces on both retirement and health programs due to their reluctance to reform Social Security. They also viewed health reform as an important step to begin to slow the rate of growth in health care costs (to "bend the health curve," as experts liked to say).

As opposed to his predecessor, Obama and his allies insisted that his own health benefit expansion include cost savings that would fully offset the benefit expansions, at least over the first decade. To meet that deficit target, they would impose higher taxes and slow the growth in other health spending. To meet the health cost containment objective, they imposed a tax on expensive health plans to create an incentive for purchasers to reduce health costs by choosing less expensive plans, and they also cut Medicare. At the same time, they created a series of pilot projects and demonstration programs through which policymakers could hopefully learn more about how to slow the growth of health care costs and later apply those findings to public programs, to the health care system at large, or to both.

Not surprisingly, the main opposition to the new bill came from what it did on the take-away side of the budget, with its Medicare cut-backs, tax increases, and efforts at a tax penalty (mandate) on individuals who did not buy health insurance.

Health reform's proponents placed great hope in its initiatives. Medicare's actuaries, however, questioned whether many of the Medicare cuts were sustainable over the long run without other reforms that would have to come later. Moreover, as confirmed by the Congressional Budget Office, the tax increases also supported a rise, not a fall, in net health spending. Because health costs were growing so quickly, because the health reform law was inherently complicated, and because it remained unclear how the law would or would not work administratively, virtually everyone expected policymakers to revisit the health system again in the coming years, even if health reform survived Republican promises to repeal it. Administrative suspicions were partly confirmed by a troubling roll-out in 2013 of a website for signing up for the new health insurance, but revisiting and fixing the law simply was not on the table as long as partisanship meant that the only fight in town could be over repeal or no repeal.

Republicans blamed Obama for the huge run-up in deficits during his first term. Their case was problematic, however. Most of the health reforms had yet to be implemented. The deep recession that Obama inherited severely reduced federal revenues as income fell across the economy and a surge in unemployment reduced the number of taxpaying households. Many of the federal programs that were designed to prop up financial institutions and industries were enacted at the end of the Bush administration. More broadly, the overwhelming share of descent from surpluses to deficits arose from the recession that had begun before Obama took office.

The Santas Leave the Stage

Just as Reagan's 1981 tax cuts likely marked the final act of the Era of Easy Financing, so did the anti-recessionary initiatives of President

Obama in 2009 and 2010 likely mark the closing moments of the Two-Santa era.

President Obama provided one possible sign of the end when he demanded that health reform abandon recent past practice and be financed through significant and controversial takeaways.

Republicans, in turn, provided another possible sign when they largely turned their attention to spending cuts—focusing for the first time in decades on the takeaway side of the budget—rather than simply more tax cuts that added to the deficit.

Yet, without understanding, much less admitting, the basic disease that the nation confronts, and by continually confounding short-run with long-run issues, both parties still focus their fights mainly on sustaining their past agendas and then, at best, trying to put salve on the deficit symptom.

The turmoil caused by deficits that rose to over $1 trillion a year in President Obama's first term, along with the rancor over health reform, led to a revolt by "Tea Party" voters within the Republican Party. As one result, Republicans successfully regained control of the House of Representatives in 2010. While the Tea Party initially focused its concern over deficits, which they blamed partly on past Republican compromises, they then moved on to social issues such as immigration reform.

Unwilling to compromise with a Democratic president and a Democratic Senate, or even with members of their own party, Tea Partiers increasingly began to threaten to shut down the government to let the nation default on its obligations to its creditors, including foreign nations. These stances probably helped President Obama to become the first Democrat since Franklin Roosevelt to win 51 percent or more of the popular vote in a second straight election, but the same fiscal fights continued into 2013.

That year witnessed a permanent extension of Bush-era tax cuts for all but the wealthiest Americans and the implementation of across-the-board "sequester" cuts (due to legislation in 2011 that supposedly would lead to an alternative and more considered reform), and then an actual shutdown of much of government in October. Following that somewhat disastrous public relations fiasco for Congress, along with slower economic growth for Americans more broadly, the House and Senate Budget committees came to a two-year budget agreement at the end of the year that almost insured no additional shut-down until after the

2016 presidential election, along with some modest deficit cuts as alternatives to additional sequestrations that were due. By some accounts, this very modest agreement was still the first bipartisan budget passed by a divided Congress in over a quarter-century.

Left out altogether in any of this legislation were the fastest growing spending programs and tax subsidies, shorter-term attention to continued high rates of unemployment, or simply fixing any program. Many Republicans could not even discuss further tax increases that could lower long-run interest costs nor reductions in tax subsidies (which operate very much like spending programs). Many Democrats could not even suggest compromise on retirement programs, even while they accept severe cuts in programs for education, children, infrastructure, and many other functions of government simply because the latter have little built-in continual growth.

Getting Beyond Our Fiscal Impasse

Through the three stages of post-World War II fiscal history that led to today's fiscal turning point, built-in spending continued to grow, reducing the fiscal freedom of policymakers even as they sought to play Santa Claus—first on one side of the budget, then the other, and then on both at the same time. As that Two-Santa era has come to an end, turmoil and rancor have risen—to no small extent because both parties largely fail to understand how we got here and because, quite simply, they compromised more easily when they either had or pretended to have money to give away.

Moving forward, simple arithmetic demands fundamental restructuring at a time when elected officials must return to the takeaway side simply to limit the unsustainable growth in debt. Consider Figure 1.1— decades of commitments by elected officials has produced a cumulative commitment that exceeds future revenues, leaving Washington to finance discretionary spending mainly by borrowing from China and other central governments as well as from institutional investors (most recently including the Federal Reserve Board) at home and abroad. Discretionary spending falls even as government revenues expand. Children and youth particularly take it on the chin, as revealed partly by cuts in educational spending and college students graduating with ever more debt.

The three previous post-war fiscal periods, and the steps that policymakers took within them, provide only limited guidance for addressing the problem at hand. The budget agreements and reforms of the Era of Fiscal Straightjackets are mere child's play compared to what we must do in the future. More than just short- and long-run fiscal policy is up for grabs, however.

Having arrived at a major fiscal turning point, we lack a structure to make programs fairer, more efficient, and more growth-oriented, and we lack consensus on how to build that structure. Each party has only recently focused on one symptom of our disease—the deficit—while each wants to retain its past victories on the spending and tax sides. Democrats fight to retain an increasingly arcane social welfare structure that is both unsustainable and increasingly directed at yesterday's problems, while Republicans say they will do anything to avoid tax increases even if that means damaging the nation's credit rating.

Even deficit-reduction after deficit reduction, as in the fiscal straightjacket era, simply cannot create the new fiscal order or flexibility needed for this great nation in the twenty-first century. Here we stand with our backs to an ocean of possibilities at a time when, despite all the economic and political turmoil, we have never been richer.

Each party is defined far more by its past than any vision for the future. But, we need such a vision if we hope to move from treating a symptom to addressing an underlying disease and, in turn, restoring the nation's historic optimism about the future and the possibilities that it offers.

5

From Controlling the Present to Controlling the Future

One recommendation stemming from [a] FAA auto-pilot study . . . is that pilots should devote more time to manual flying, rather than relying on automated systems, so they are better prepared at recognizing the warning signs of an emergency. "We're forgetting how to fly," explained the committee co-chair, a pilot himself.

—Lenwood Brooks[1]

The conversion of Keynesian and supply-side theories into political apologies for most giveaways, along with the rising activism of both political parties, explains a lot about how we arrived at our current fiscal state. But knowing about these trends does not convey the enormity of the challenge that we face. The truly troubling aspect of this crisis is the expanding drive of both political parties to extend giveaways and activist control not just to the present, but the future as well.

In the previous chapter, we noted the increasing tendency of presidents and Congresses to enact permanent and automatically growing programs. In this chapter, we discuss the profound consequences when elected officials shift resources from efforts to solve their current problems, such as unemployment during a recession or Depression (the main thrust of New Deal policies), toward permanent and automatic growth in programs that are designed never to fully solve anything but only provide ever-increasing comfort and security (the main thrust of today's social policies).

From Annual to Eternal Budgets

Let us begin with the basics. Federal spending comes in two basic varieties: discretionary and mandatory. For discretionary spending, the president and Congress decide each year which programs to fund, which new ones to create, and which old ones to kill. To do so, they enact twelve appropriations bills that, today, fund the defense budget and a wide range of domestic programs in many areas—from education to environmental protection, from biomedical research to food safety, from transportation to border security, and so on. Congress must vote to fund most of these programs every year.

For mandatory spending, the president and Congress create programs (mainly "entitlements") that continue automatically from year to year, unless policymakers enact laws in later years to change them. These entitlements have increasingly dominated federal spending. President Franklin Roosevelt worked with Congress to create Social Security in 1935, the first major spending entitlement, while President Lyndon Johnson, who sought to expand the New Deal into the Great Society, worked with Congress to create Medicare and Medicaid in 1965. As they created these and other entitlement programs over the years—Food Stamps, unemployment insurance, the Earned Income Tax Credit, disability insurance, civilian and military retirement programs, Supplemental Security Income, and others—policymakers expanded many that were already in place.

They also designed a number of them, particularly in retirement and health, to grow automatically forever by annually providing more generous benefits to more eligible people. To top it off, these automatic growth rates, particularly in retirement and health programs, were sometimes set at levels above the growth rate in people's private incomes and the economy itself.

To Social Security, for instance, elected officials added large numbers of eligible workers in 1950; created disability insurance and reduced the age at which women were eligible for benefits in 1956; lowered the eligibility age for men in 1961; enacted large benefit increases in the late 1960s and early 1970s (including a 20 percent increase in 1972); and established automatic cost-of-living adjustments starting in 1975. In 1972, they created Supplemental Security Income and, very importantly, made growth in real Social Security benefits automatic from one generation to the next. To Medicare, they added prescription drug coverage in 2003.[2]

Naturally, entitlements as a whole grew much faster than discretionary programs, gradually consuming an ever-larger share of total federal spending.[3] Entitlements swelled from slightly less than 30 percent of spending in the early 1960s to nearly 60 percent by 2013, while discretionary programs shrunk from 68 percent to 35 percent of federal spending over the same period. Over just twenty years, mandatory spending grew from 10.8 percent of GDP in 1993 to 13.6 percent of GDP in 2013.[4]

A simple reason for the power of mandatory programs is the politics of cutting programs, which always raises the ire of voters. Budget insiders calculate that entitlements and tax subsidies are "cut" if policymakers simply reduce promised benefits—even if average benefits continue to grow after the "cut." An appropriation is "cut" if it merely fails to keep pace with inflation.

Despite government's expanding scope, particularly during the Depression and its aftermath, policymakers often brought discretionary spending in line simply by failing to appropriate new increases. Revenues would then grow with the economy and spending temporarily would not. They never applied such constraint to entitlements as a whole.

To be sure, some entitlements, though permanent in nature, had little or no built-in growth, and policymakers even cut entitlements on occasion—for instance, in 1983 when they pared Social Security benefits to rescue the program from potential insolvency or in several years when they cut reimbursements to Medicare providers. Welfare reform in 1996 removed Aid to Families with Dependent Children (AFDC) from permanent entitlement status but, by that time, AFDC had paled in relative significance, mainly because benefit levels did not keep pace with wages or incomes.

Despite these occasional efforts to rein in their costs, in the end, growth in entitlement benefits and in eligible recipients far outstripped those efforts.

Meanwhile, a parallel phenomenon unfolded on the tax side. There, policymakers allocated to individuals and corporations an ever-growing array of deductions, credits, and other write-offs known collectively as "tax expenditures." Most tax expenditures, like entitlements, remain in effect unless policymakers enact laws to change them. Acting essentially like a hidden form of government spending, they now cost the federal government an estimated $1.2 trillion or about 7 percent of GDP in lost revenue each year.[5] Reined in briefly from 1982 to 1986, largely to pay for a reduction in tax rates, they have since resumed their large growth.

Policymakers often dismiss tax expenditures as "loopholes," but the costliest among them are about a dozen that provide tax benefits for tens of millions of households, making them as important to many Americans as Social Security, Medicare, and Medicaid. They include the tax-free treatment of employer-provided health care; the home mortgage interest deduction; deductions for charitable contributions; and special treatment for capital gains, 401(k) plans, and other investment earnings.[6] Almost all of the largest tax expenditures are not merely permanent, but also grow from year to year.

As entitlements and tax expenditures grow regardless of changing societal needs, they require more spending, drain revenues, and reduce fiscal freedom. Eventually, the prospect of new and growing future deficits arises even in the absence of any new congressional action. At this fiscal turning point, the decision of policymakers simply to let mandatory spending grow automatically typically outweighs all of their deficit-cutting actions on the discretionary side.

Current and future red ink is just one symptom of a larger problem—Congress's lack of control over the budget—and continual deficit reduction agreements such as those of the fiscal straightjacket period from 1982 to 1997 ultimately fail even to stop the red ink, much less redirect the budget toward new priorities. Setting more animal traps cannot fully remove unwanted critters in a house with its doors wide open.

As we consider where we have been and where we are going, we must also recognize that policymakers have never reformed these programs adequately to accommodate another powerful economic force: the demographic changes that only now are starting to dramatically reduce the number of taxpayers per beneficiary of not just retirement and health programs, but of all programs. We are at the front end of the retirement of "baby boomers," the generation of Americans who were born between 1946 and 1964. They began retiring in droves in 2008, as the oldest of them started becoming eligible for "early retirement" benefits under Social Security at age 62 and became eligible for Medicare three years later at age 65. Their retirement will affect the budget in two

Figure 5.1. *Federal Social Security, Medicare, and Medicaid Outlays, 1940–2088, as percentage of GDP*

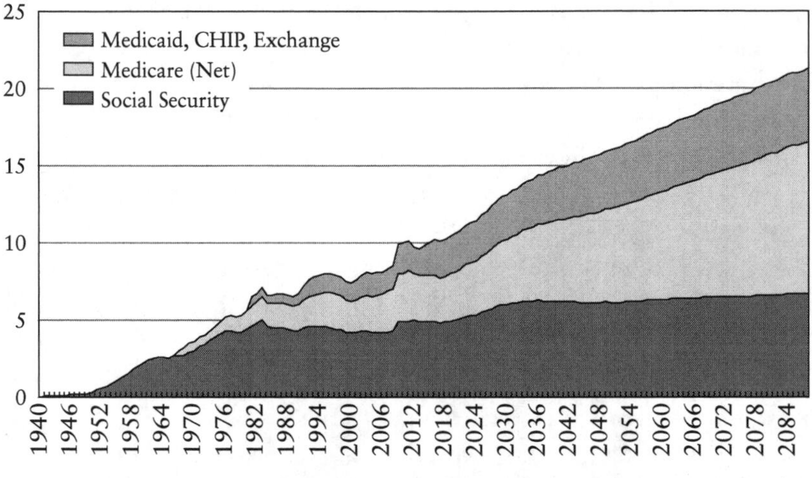

Source: Author's compilation of data from OMB Historical Tables and the Congressional Budget Office. Projections assume that scheduled cuts in Medicare payment rates to physicians and other cost-control mechanisms in health care programs do not take full effect.

major ways—by driving Social Security and Medicare benefit costs up, and pushing income and payroll tax revenues down as these workers exit the workforce.

Social Security, Medicare, and Medicaid (close to half of which goes toward long-term care) dominate the modern history of domestic government (see Figure 5.1). With rare exception they have grown as a share of GDP ever since Roosevelt created Social Security in the 1930s, and they are projected to continue growing automatically in this way for as far as one can see.

Were all three of these programs fully financed by simple, transparent taxes such as the Social Security payroll tax, rather than financed by multiple taxes and deficit spending, the tax rate required to support them would be about double the percentage of GDP that they now consume. Thus, when spending on these programs was about 2 percent of GDP, about a four–percentage-point tax on Social Security earnings would have been required to fund the programs in their entirety. Today, at about 10 percent of GDP, they would require a 20 percent tax rate. Projections showing that spending on Social Security, Medicare, and Medicaid will reach 20 percent of GDP would mean about a 40 percent tax rate *for these programs alone.*

Figure 5.2. *Expected Social Security and Medicare Benefits for a Two-Earner Couple Earning the Average Wage, in 2013 dollars*

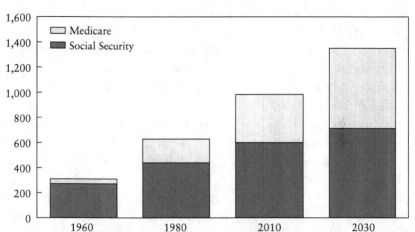

Source: C. Eugene Steuerle and Caleb Quakenbush, "Social Security and Medicare Taxes and Benefits over a Lifetime: 2013 Update," Washington, D.C., The Urban Institute, 2013.

The growth in these programs is reflected in the value of the lifetime benefits that an average-wage couple would receive at age 65. Compare, for instance, these benefits with how much would be needed in an Individual Retirement Account (IRA) or other account at age 65 to pay the benefits for an average couple. For a couple retiring in about 1960, that figure would have been just over $300,000 in today's dollars. For one retiring in 2010, it is about $1 million ($985,000). For one retiring around 2035, it is about $1.35 million. Nor do those figures include the old age support that many receive if they end up in nursing homes, where most turn to Medicaid to cover their costs when they remain there for any lengthy period.[7]

Social Security, Medicare, and Medicaid are not the only retirement and health programs that are growing on either the spending or tax sides. Other growing items include tax subsidies for health insurance and, on the state and local levels, public employee pension plans, which faced greater public scrutiny after the Great Recession of 2008–09 forced states to recognize, at least in part, that these plans were severely underfunded.[8]

What causes all this growth? Basically, retirement programs automatically spend ever-larger shares of our GDP due to (1) benefits that increase automatically as wages increase, (2) ever-more years of support as people live longer, and (3) the decline in taxpayers relative to beneficiaries when birth rates fall. In health care, the growth largely comes from some of the same demographic pressures and from the cost pressures that derive from a key feature of most health insurance: allowing patients and doctors to decide what everyone else will pay. No other government programs provide such open-ended and essentially uncontrolled entitlement (see Table 5.1).

Many other programs also contain built-in growth. Take some permanent tax subsidies. Like spending on health and retirement, their cost has grown year after year, independent of any public judgment on changing priorities and needs. For example, pension subsidies have grown to over $150 billion per year, even though they have done little to protect the vast majority of workers. Health subsidies in the tax system grow rapidly, like other health expenses. The largest of all tax expenditures, costing over $200 billion per year, is the exclusion from income and Social Security tax of compensation received by workers as health insurance. As an open-ended exclusion, it is worth more to higher-income taxpayers, because they typically receive more expensive insurance and would face the higher tax rates were such income taxable. Housing subsidies grow year after year, rising as Americans take out larger and larger mortgages. These subsidies also mostly benefit wealthy homeowners, who tend to purchase larger houses and can apply the mortgage interest deduction at a higher tax rate; they deliver less to low- and moderate-income households.[9]

The swelling costs described above are not limited to the federal government, either. A similar crisis is unfolding among state and local budgets. Due to rising enrollment and open-ended health budgets, states' Medicaid spending now rivals their spending on K–12 education, which has declined as a share of state spending and even declined in real terms in some years following the Great Recession. State and local pension plans have amassed large, underfunded obligations to government employees, in addition to health benefits promised to retirees. While state tax bases have eroded for a variety of reasons, measures such as exempting pension income from income taxation or limits on property taxes, which favor older (and often wealthier) citizens and incumbent homeowners, have not helped.[10]

Table 5.1. *Primary Sources of Automatic Growth in Retirement and Health Programs*

Higher annual benefits for succeeding cohorts of retirees	Retirement benefits in traditional plans are scheduled to grow so that if your wages are 30 percent higher than those of your parents, you will receive 30 percent higher annual benefits.
Ever more years of support	With minor exceptions, the age for receiving benefits stays constant or rises at a slower rate than life expectancy. Thus, an individual receives benefits for ever-more years and ever-larger portions of his or her life. A couple retiring at age 62 will soon be entitled on average to about thirty years of benefits. That is, one or the other of the spouses is increasingly likely to live at least to age 90.
Falling birth rates	A decline in the birth rate adds to the decline in the worker-retiree ratio and taxpayer-to-beneficiary ratio supporting all government programs, not just Social Security. For decades in America, and in many other countries, much of the long-term impact on spending relative to revenues was offset by the increase in workers (and the taxes they paid) as women and baby boomers entered the workforce. Those days are gone.
Open-ended health programs	Patients and doctors together bear limited financial consequence for their decisions. The costs for care are shifted mainly to others in our insurance system or taxpayers. At no or very low cost, our demand is close to infinite, and so is the supply of health care services. Almost all government health insurance programs grow automatically to accommodate new discoveries, drugs, and methods, not to mention science's rising ability to identify diseases and disabilities, both physical and mental.[a]

Moreover, health care has been considered a "superior good." That is, as we become richer, we demand that an increasing share of what we consume be in the form of health services. Consequently, a faster-rising economy leads to an even-larger increase in the demand for health care. Even in countries with government attempts to regulate the entire health sector (through more global constraints), controlling health cost growth has proven difficult.[b] |

a Carlo Cottarelli and Michael Keen, 2010, "Fiscal Policies and Growth: Constraints and Opportunities," Manuscript, Washington, DC: IMF.

b I. C. André Joumard and C. Nicq, "Health Care Systems: Efficiency and Institutions", *OECD Economics Department Working Papers*, No. 769, OECD Publishing, 2010.

Why Keynesian and Supply-Side Apologists Could Be Almost Right in the Past and Clearly Wrong Now

Even though policymakers over-emphasized the application of Keynesian and supply-side theories to support their giveaway policies, the stakes were not that high as long as they were fighting over the present, not the future. But, that is not true of our current situation.

Throughout the nation's first two centuries, spending was mainly discretionary and revenues grew each year as the economy expanded. As a result, the budget would always generate surpluses over the long run as long as policymakers merely continued their current policies. (Figure 5.3 illustrates the point.) Consequently, policymakers could use these potentially available surpluses to spend more or cut taxes according to the needs of the time or the whims of voters. Elected officials did not necessarily have to rescind a past promise that spending would grow or raise taxes before they could do anything new.[11] In fact, most of the time, they actually had to increase spending or cut taxes simply to avoid the fiscal problems or "drag" that those future surpluses would have generated.[12]

Let us say, for instance, that revenues grow at 3 percent a year, while spending into the future is flat. In less than a quarter of a century, policymakers would have about half of all future revenues to allocate for new purposes. Even that example probably understates the earlier fiscal freedom of policymakers. Most likely, the amount of discretionary spending that was obligated into the future would shrink (rather than

Figure 5.3. *Traditional Budget Scenario: Flat or Declining Spending*

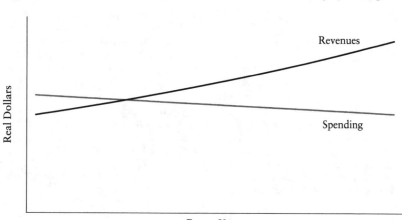

remain flat). Discretionary spending growth was seldom built in, certainly not on an eternal basis.[13] In addition, progressive tax systems were not yet adjusted for inflation, so revenues rose significantly faster than incomes as taxpayers moved into higher brackets.[14]

The bottom line, then, is this; throughout the nation's history, only recently has spending been scheduled to rise faster than revenues on a permanent basis. Today, unlike before, any new spending increase or tax cut—including those that the nation might consider to address an economic slowdown—cannot be offset down the road by future expected revenue growth.

This simple historical change in the structure of fiscal policy drives much of the fiscal anguish and confusion that permeates all or almost all developed nations. Where policymakers of the past could achieve budget balance simply by enacting few or no increases in discretionary spending for a while, or in a few cases (mainly after war) cutting discretionary spending, such a strategy would prove futile in today's fiscal context.

Can higher economic growth fuel a much higher growth in revenues, reducing future-year deficits? Some liberals like to claim so, suggesting that they may not need to reform programs like Social Security after all. Some conservatives, too, like to claim so, arguing that tax cuts always pay for themselves through the economic growth that they purportedly create.

In reality, in today's environment, economic growth provides only limited gains. It does boost revenues relative to scheduled discretionary

Figure 5.4. *Today's Budget Scenario: Built-in Growth in Spending*

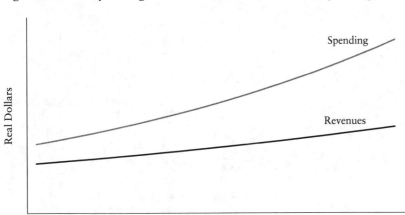

spending (Figure 5.5). But, the largest and most important growing programs are designed so that when the economy grows faster, they grow faster as well (Figure 5.6). Thus, economic growth means that spending automatically increases along with revenues, which does little to alleviate our problem.

As we shall see next, all of that entails an array of economic and political consequences that we can neither define nor solve simply by focusing on deficits.

Figure 5.5. *Idealized Budget Scenario: Faster Growth Leads to More Revenues in Future Years*

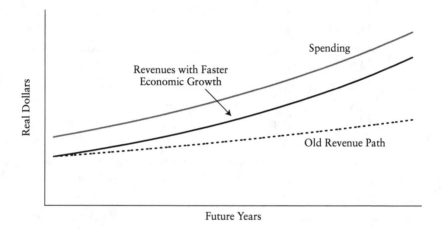

Figure 5.6. *Why Growth Is Not Enough: Expenditures Are Designed to Increase with Economic Growth, Too*

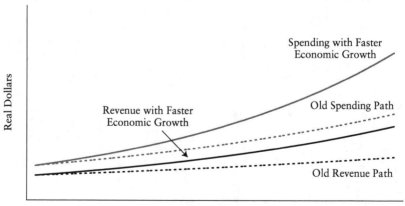

6

The Four Deadly Economic Consequences

I am convinced we have now passed the worst and with continued unity of effort we shall rapidly recover. There is one certainty of the future of a people of the resources, intelligence and character of the people of the United States—that is, prosperity.

—President Herbert Hoover, May 1, 1930

Our fiscal disease is deadly, for both economic and political reasons. To understand how, think of our nation as a biological species, one that has expanded and grown. If a species grows faster than its food supplies, it can enter a period of crisis, in which it not only starves some of its members, but also consumes the very seeds that are supposed to provide for future nourishment. The United States, along with much of the developed world, is following a fiscal policy that is draining the economic and political nutrients on which we depend. In this and the next chapter, I will show how this disease threads together seven deadly consequences—four economic and three political—that are typically left unconnected in public debates, particularly during election time.

Over the past several decades, what began as legitimate concerns for expanding social welfare, Keynesian concerns about maintaining demand in a recession, and supply-side concerns about eliminating disincentives to work and saving have since given the nation's leaders the intellectual ammunition to increasingly commit future federal resources to fast-growing programs that are already in place. By establishing and expanding these efforts, our leaders helped bring a 200-year-plus period of fiscal policymaking to an end—a period in which, other than during war or national emergency, revenues would grow fast enough to finance a rising stream of giveaways in the form of spending increases and tax cuts. In fact, especially after government had grown large after World War II, more legislated giveaways were often required to avoid a "fiscal drag" on the economy that rising surpluses would have nourished.

Now, the reverse is true. Built-in growth in spending will exceed the growth in revenue forever—or until the economy collapses. Eventually, with revenues completely allotted to finance fast-growing entitlements (as they were temporarily for the first time in 2009), Congress will have to finance any dollar of discretionary spending by borrowing, often from abroad.

Consequently, we now confront four deadly economic consequences: (1) rising and unsustainable levels of debt; (2) a shrinking ability to fight recession or meet other emergencies; (3) a budget for a declining nation that invests ever less in its future, particularly in children and youth; and (4) broken government, as reflected in antiquated tax and social welfare systems. All derive from the decades-long effort by each political party to control the future before the other does.

Fortunately, unlike problems such as terrorism or disease or natural catastrophe, these four economic consequences are all self-imposed. Thus, we have the power to address them. Unfortunately, the steps to do so will impose significant political costs on any officials courageous enough to try.

Consequence 1: Economic Decline from Rising and Unsustainable Levels of Debt

The Congressional Budget Office (CBO), a key arm of Congress, prepares a long-term projection each year of what would happen if we stay on the current budgetary path. Figure 6.1 illustrates the type of result that CBO has been projecting year after year.

Of course, nothing like it would ever come to pass. At some point before debt ever reached such hypothetically projected levels, we would find ourselves without the lenders to continue to feed our fiscal appetite. That is because, as former Federal Reserve Board Chairman Ben Bernanke warned almost throughout his tenure, lenders do not continue to lend to borrowers who make no effort to address their debt problems. That is true for a family that wants to borrow more

Figure 6.1. *The U.S. Federal Debt, as a percentage of GDP*

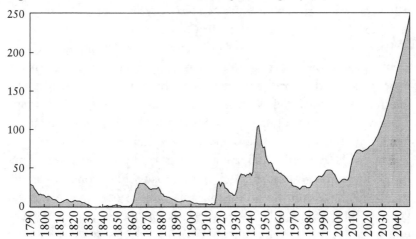

Source: Data from Congressional Budget Office, *2013 Long Term Budget Outlook*. Projections use the alternative fiscal scenario, which assumes that policymakers maintain current Medicare payment rates to physicians and extend certain expiring tax provisions.

from a local bank, or a country that wants to borrow more from its residents or its lenders overseas.

Moreover, even before reaching that borrowing end point, the nation could face an economic crisis as lenders begin to lose confidence and, as a result, demand higher rates of return on their investments—that is, higher interest rates. Their loss of confidence could send the dollar plummeting on global markets, which would send inflation soaring and force even higher interest rates, which would cause the dollar to fall even further in a vicious cycle that would severely weaken the economy.[1]

Nations that face exploding debt levels or the kind of problems outlined above often refuse to pay their debts and declare bankruptcy. Because so many nations depend upon the U.S. dollar to stabilize world financial markets, a U.S. default could prompt not just a U.S. crisis, but a global depression. U.S. government bonds and bills have long served as the go-to safety vehicle for investors. A U.S. default would shake the global economy to its core because it would signal that U.S. bonds and bills are no longer the rock-solid investments on which investors around the world have long relied.[2]

No one knows when the day of reckoning may arrive—the day when lenders might refuse to lend us any more money, or the day when they get nervous enough to demand a higher rate of return on their lending, or when higher interest rates cascade into a cycle of a plummeting dollar, soaring inflation, and a weakened economy.

However, one must not infer too much from short-term trends. While recovery from the Great Recession has been much slower than many experts expected, nourishing pessimism, above-average growth is normal for most recoveries because of unused potential in the economy. Thus, we should continue to expect short-term periods of both faster and slower economic growth than any projection would suggest.[3]

Even without a day of reckoning or crisis, rising debt poses huge limitations on what government, and, more broadly, the economy can do. Rising debt levels imply that ever-larger shares of our income and our government spending will go to pay interest on that debt, much of which today goes to foreign governments, many of which are not friendly to us. Rising interest rates or a lack of economic confidence tends to reduce private investment, which in turn reduces growth rates even in absence of outright recession or depression.

The Quickening Debt

The problem of rising deficits and debt has become far more apparent in the early years of the twenty-first century. In the United States, as we saw in the Chapter 4, officials transformed the surpluses in years between 1998 and 2001 into a new round of giveaways, with large tax cuts and sizable increases in both defense and domestic spending. Then, baby boomers began to retire in mass numbers starting in 2008, imposing an expected but nevertheless significant burden on Social Security, Medicare, and, to some degree, Medicaid that will cumulate for over two decades. In more recent years, Republican lawmakers fought to make permanent all of the tax cuts that were enacted on a temporary basis earlier in this century under President George W. Bush, while Democrats sought to make *almost* all of them permanent. The result at the beginning of President Obama's second term was an end only to those cuts for couples making more than $450,000 a year and singles making more than $400,000. Also in the early years of the Obama presidency, officials of both parties boosted spending through wars in Afghanistan and Iraq, enacted a large stimulus measure in 2009 to revive the economy, cut payroll taxes in 2011 and 2012, and expanded health subsidies for both elderly and non-elderly Americans.

Figure 6.1 presents a picture unlike any in our history. From 2001 to 2014, federal debt held by the public rose from 32.5 percent to 76 percent of GDP. Projections generally show it recovering slightly once the economy returns to its potential, and then rising beyond those levels during the 2020s.[4] The point is not simply that debt has peaked at a level higher than any time other than during World War II because of both the recession and the profligate period that preceded it. At no other time in our history has projected future debt done anything but fall rapidly after the emergency of the day—war or recession—ended. By contrast, tomorrow's growing level of debt to GDP results directly from the declining fiscal freedom displayed in many ways throughout this book.

The scenario outlined in Figure 6.1 is just that—a scenario. It reflects our best sense of what the future may bring if current policy would continue, debt would grow, and the economy would return more toward normal economic growth. But, of course, it drastically understates our problems simply because high and potentially rising debt at some point can take a heavy toll on the economy in ways that are not reflected in the scenario. Having said that, policymakers may come to their senses and take the necessary steps to prevent this scenario from becoming a reality. Because much of the growth in debt in later years comes from nothing more than the ever-rising and compounding levels of interest payments on the debt, an effort by policymakers to address the underlying problem of rising red ink could improve the situation profoundly.

As I have emphasized, the long-term deficit is but one symptom of our greater problems, just as weight loss can be one symptom of cancer. While I am fairly optimistic that elected officials will at least continue to bring the nation back from the brink of economic collapse, that is ultimately a futile effort if policymakers do not address the underlying fiscal cancer itself—futile in no small part because of the other deadly consequences.

Consequence 2: Less Ability to Combat Recession and Address New Emergencies

Due to its length and severity, the Great Recession nourished a belief in some circles that the federal government cannot successfully rejuvenate a weakened economy. After all, President George W. Bush and Congress enacted the Troubled Assets Relief Program (TARP), a $700 billion effort to prop up the nation's sputtering financial sector, while President

Obama and Congress enacted a huge stimulus measure of tax cuts and spending increases in early 2009, totaling an estimated $787 billion at its birth. While unemployment later rose, nonpartisan experts like the economists at the Congressional Budget Office concluded that the stimulus measure actually worked—that the recession would have lasted longer and unemployment would have risen more without it. But, that did little to silence the critics.

Nevertheless, policymakers must retain the ability to conduct countercyclical economic policy by allowing revenues to fall and spending to increase to prevent recessions from spiraling out of control. Sometimes, the government is the only significant entity with the power to revive an economy that is stuck in neutral or worse. Monetary policy has its limits, in part because it cannot push nominal interest rates below zero and real interest rates much below that without inducing inflation. In the absence of programs that expand in recessions and contract in periods of growth, as well as other federal interventions, economies are left to cure themselves, which often prolongs a downturn and extends human suffering unnecessarily.

Government already has a range of important tax and spending programs in place that kick in automatically during recessions. On the tax side, the tax code as a whole is strongly countercyclical; businesses and households earn more and pay more when times are good, and they earn less and pay less when times are bad. On the spending side, individuals have access to a range of benefits during recessions, such as unemployment compensation when they lose their jobs, SNAP (food stamps) to help them feed their families, and Medicaid to provide health insurance when they fall into poverty.

Ideally, policymakers would not only maintain these automatic mechanisms but strengthen them as well. Politically, however, elected officials want to do more than sit and watch some set of automatically countercyclical measures already in place work their will. They want to take additional action—if only to show their constituents that they are on the job, attuned to the suffering back home, and ready to deploy federal resources to address it. Whatever the economic arguments, that is a major political reason why, during recessions, they create measures to supplement those already in place, such as temporary tax cuts or spending on job-creating infrastructure projects. In modern activist times, no Republican or Democratic president has failed to take such actions.

Fiscally, that is fine as long as policymakers take advantage of good times to reduce debt-to-GDP levels. With a debt-to-GDP level in place that does not threaten economic harm, and with long-term revenues rising faster than spending pre-ordained from the past, policymakers have the flexibility—the fiscal freedom—to cut taxes and boost spending during bad times (thus sending deficits temporarily higher).

Look again at Figure 6.1, but this time, focus on World War II and the decades immediately after. Economists often point to wartime spending for proof that counter-cyclical policy works. After all, it was the huge increase in military spending that ended the Great Depression once and for all. But they pay a lot less attention to the later period. Over the nearly three decades that followed World War II—through recoveries and recessions—policymakers managed to shrink the debt-to-GDP level by an average of about 2.5 percentage points of GDP per year (and at a higher average rate in non-recession years). Economic growth and inflation added to GDP much faster than deficits added to debt. In fact, that ratio fell almost every single year from 1946 to 1974, even as policymakers enacted a steady stream of tax cuts and spending increases. Put simply, policymakers could enact short-term stimulus measures during this period and later because the budget was under control over the long run.

By the time that the Great Recession hit in late 2007, policymakers had already driven the budget back into the red (after the surpluses of 1998 through 2001) through a combination of tax cuts, war spending, and new prescription drug coverage for Medicare (though a short recession in 2001 also played a role). The turn from surplus to deficit since the end of the previous century was already the most remarkable in the nation's history. Thus, by 2007, policymakers had already been struggling with a rising debt-to-GDP ratio for most of the decade even before the economy began to sink.

Moving forward, a high debt-to-GDP ratio that is projected to grow higher still will further constrain policymakers who seek countercyclical measures during a downturn. Moreover, the economic effects of rising debt will weaken the power of any stimulus that they enact since true stimulus requires an increase, not maintenance, of government activity from any starting level. Creditors may grow wary, and rating agencies may further downgrade U.S. debt. (Standard & Poor's took this step in August of 2011 when it downgraded federal debt from AAA to AA+.

Different agencies formally threatened further downgrades in later years if some Republicans had gained credibility that they could sustain threats to not pay obligations to bondholders.)

Even if they accept that countercyclical policy makes sense, politicians who confront high and rising debt become more reluctant to act to raise it further still. When they see debt rising or falling little in a recovery, they raise even more doubts about the effectiveness of stimulus. This combination of economic and political forces had already made it difficult for them to provide further stimulus in the United States in the slow growth years immediately following the Great Recession. It also led many other developed nations to undergo what many, including me, view as unreasonable short-term belt-tightening. Thus, for the foreseeable future, it is highly likely that policymakers will fail to respond to another severe recession by enacting appropriate stimulus measures. That, in turn, will likely prolong future downturns while keeping unemployment unnecessarily high.

Policymakers often group this consequence of a declining ability to fight combat recession or other emergencies along with the consequence of rising and unsustainable levels of debt, discussing both of them under the rubric of "deficits"—even though the first mainly involves short-run, counter-cyclical policy, and the second involves long-run policy. But these two deadly consequences are very different from one another, and policymakers should not confuse them. Long-term deficits that reach unsustainable levels threaten economic crisis and drain a nation's economic strength over time. Short-term deficits can cushion the blow of a recession, but an already high debt-to-GDP ratio will constrain our ability to conduct such robust counter-cyclical policy.

Consider, again, the post-World War II period. Policymakers spent the requisite amount on defense to ensure that the United States could lead the Allies to victory, sending deficits and debt much higher in the short term, but they also prepared for the future. They raised taxes for the longer term and scheduled spending cuts (as when the troops came home) that nourished projections of long-term surpluses and a falling debt-to-GDP ratio. Meanwhile, they had enacted little built-in growth in future spending. At this writing, the U.S. economic and fiscal situation cries out for a similar balancing act. Policymakers need to enact temporary tax cuts and spending increases when and if the economy keeps struggling, but that short-term policy becomes much more viable economically and politically when they have in place a long-term budget that allows revenues to rise significantly faster than spending as an economy strengthens.

Consequence 3: Budget for a Declining Nation

The president and Congress may well move us back from the brink of collapse. So, let us presume that policymakers do enough to avoid the first two of our deadly economic consequences, taking enough steps to stem the rise of debt and ensure that government has the flexibility to respond to recessions.

That would be no small feat, and it would take us far beyond the dysfunctional governing of today. Unfortunately, that would still not take us where we need to go. Once again, the disease is not the rising deficits and debt; that is but a symptom to treat.

Even if we eliminate the first two of our deadly economic consequences, we are still not out of the woods. The disease, the loss of fiscal freedom due to excessive efforts to control the future, still leaves us with a budget for a declining nation, with three closely related long-term threats:

- ever-smaller shares of our national income devoted to children;
- ever-smaller shares of our national income devoted to government investments; and
- government programs intended to promote economic mobility, or a better life for ourselves and our children, that often do just the opposite for those who are disadvantaged to begin with.

These threats will remain even if we build a budget that somehow reaches sustainability and does not explode, even one that further contains the means to adjust to economic downturns. Moreover, these threats can perpetuate a vicious downward spiral, as when private investment increasingly goes abroad due to a real or relative decline in education, knowledge, and skill level at home.

Spending for children and investment has been on the cutting-room floor for quite some time. Take the budget that President Obama typically proposed in his early years, even before spending cuts and sequesters began to dominate fiscal policy in Washington. While progressives hailed his budget, it did not significantly address any of these declining nation issues. Its largest proposed long-term spending increase was not for education or infrastructure or any other investment that would pay off in higher living standards down the road. It was for interest on the debt that earlier generations and the recession had run up. The largest increases in all of his budgets, whether newly proposed or simply scheduled largely by the hands of dead and retired legislators, was devoted to the retirement and health programs. The non-child portions of Social Security, Medicare, and Medicaid remain slated to grow much faster than the economy because of their built-in growth factors, combined with population aging and a health cost growth that continues to outstrip inflation.

The rest of the budget would shrink, a fact about which Obama's former budget director, Peter Orszag, once wrote approvingly on his official blog. Early on, he noted that under Obama's fiscal blueprint, domestic discretionary spending—which provides the funds for education and infrastructure and a host of other investments—would fall to its lowest level as a share of the economy since 1962.[5] Since then, Congress has moved even more aggressively to cut these discretionary programs.

These troubling trends deserve a closer look.

Crumbs for Children

Children are a priority in every family budget. From the moment we hold our newborns in our arms, we worry about how best to feed, clothe, house, and educate them, and we sacrifice other priorities so as not to shortchange our kids. But in the federal budget, the opposite is true. As a nation, we allot only a small fraction of spending to children. And that fraction will continue to fall as long as both parties refuse to address the underlying trends that plague our spending and tax systems.

Colleagues from the Urban Institute and I have been tracking federal spending and investment in children for several years through the Annie E. Casey Foundation for First Focus and the Foundation for Child Development. We have studied budget patterns since 1960 as well as projections for the next ten years (based on current law).

We have found that kids have never batted first in the budget. In 1960, when defense took about half of the budget pie, the share of the remaining domestic budget allotted to children was at best about 20 percent. Between 1960 and 2010, while the domestic piece of the budget grew significantly—largely due to economic growth and a

Table 6.1. *Share of Projected Growth in Federal Outlays from 2012 to 2023 Going to Children and Other Major Budget Items*

Major budget items	Difference between 2012 Outlays and Projected 2023 Outlays (billions 2012 dollars)	Share of Change in Outlays
Social Security, Medicare, and Medicaid (excluding children)	$780	66%
Interest on the debt	$444	37%
Defense	($106)	–9%
Children	20	2%
All other outlays	$50	4%
Total growth	$1,189	100%

Notes: Numbers may not sum to totals because of rounding. Social Security, Medicare, and Medicaid category excludes spending already captured as part of children's spending.

Source: Julia Isaacs et al., *Kids' Share 2013: Federal Expenditures on Children in 2012 and Future Projections* (Washington, D.C.: Urban Institute, 2013). Authors' estimates based on data from the *Budget of the U.S. Government Fiscal Year 2014* and Congressional Budget Office projections.

declining share for defense—children still got only about 10 percent to 16 percent of growth. To be sure, they got some of this expanding domestic pie, even if a smaller share of the total. When policymakers shifted close to $1.5 trillion a year (in today's dollars) from defense to domestic spending after the Korean War, children received a bit of that domestic addition, particularly in means-tested programs.[6]

But, now, pressures to reduce spending are strongest especially on the very types of programs on which children rely—domestic discretionary programs such as education that do not grow automatically. Even before recent deficit reduction agreements began to significantly constrain discretionary spending for years to come, we projected that children would get just two percent of the $1 trillion or so more of *additional spending* that the federal government would undertake in 2023 over and above 2012 (see Table 6.1). Adopt any of the leading Republican or Democratic plans to reduce deficits even more and the figures only get worse. This downward path in the share of spending on kids was established quite some time ago and it did not change much when Democrats regained control of Congress in 2007, when Democrats regained the White House in 2009, or when Republicans recaptured the House of Representatives in 2011.

What is driving the projections?

Let us assume that we have normal economic growth over the next decade. That will generate about 35 percent more revenue over that period. Revenues tend to rise at about the same rate as the economy. More revenues mean more opportunities.

A sizable share of those added revenues, however, will do nothing more than pay more interest on the debt as it keeps compounding. Meanwhile, a stronger economy down the road will gradually send interest rates higher. Still, annual revenue increases of the size described above normally would leave a fair amount of money to finance additional domestic and defense spending. Retirement and health programs, however, claim so much of the additional funds for the domestic budget that everything else gets a smaller share—and, in many programs, no share at all.

Children's programs will be among those hit the hardest. Children's spending will fall sharply as a share of the economy, from 2.2 percent of GDP in 2012 to 1.8 percent in 2023, pushing spending on children below pre-recession levels. In 2017, Washington will start spending more on interest payments than children. The only category of spending on children that is projected to increase is health care, and that is not necessarily good news. Much of the spending goes just to cover the rising costs of an out-of-control health budget, and children represent only a tiny share of the health budget anyway.

These skewed priorities defy reason as well as fairness. In per-person terms in 2008, the federal government spent $3,822 on children and $26,355 on the elderly (in 2011 dollars). Take into account state and local spending, and a child on average still only gets about 45 percent as much as an elderly person, and the gap between their levels of spending only increases in the future. As the children's share of the budget shrinks and we invest proportionately less in them, we cannot expect them in later years to earn the money that will enable them to pay the taxes to cover our ballooning pile of retirement and health benefits. In essence, we have codified into the law the following rule for the young: they owe us ever more when they become adults, and we owe them ever less while they remain children.

Children will always take an increasingly cramped back seat as long as we adults assume the front seat and then roll our seat backward to stretch our legs. Our budget will spend more on each generation of adults as we approach retirement, while leaving the costs to our children and grandchildren. They deserve better.

Investing Less

Children are not alone. Dollars are declining for investments of all sorts. Even the supposed big build-up in infrastructure spending in the "stimulus" packages of 2009 and 2010 was scheduled to end dramatically and quickly.

In a study before the Great Recession, several Urban Institute researchers looked at what was happening to "investment"—which includes traditional measures in things like plants and equipment, and some items that go to children, such as education. It does not include, however, some items for children that were included in the analysis above, including many social welfare programs.[7]

Like the children's budget, the investment budget has been shrinking as a share of the domestic budget (although it retained some absolute growth). As for the future, education and work supports would decline in both absolute and relative terms under most projections. Only social supports that might be defined as "investments" would grow in absolute but not relative terms—and even that growth is due entirely to greater health spending.

Policymakers enacted a temporary increase in infrastructure spending and support for state and local education spending as part of a 2009 stimulus measure. Those increases, however, were only temporary, and the investment budget has returned to a negative track as these spending efforts unwind. Moreover, the temporary boost in federal spending on education was not large enough to offset a decline in state and local spending on education.[8]

Budget officials track the relative and sometimes absolute decline in federal investment outlays (excluding work and social supports) as part of the president's budget each year. President Obama and many of his advisors argued that the federal government should promote investment. But rhetoric does not mean reality. In his 2012 budget, for instance, the president and his advisers pushed rhetorically for more investment but monetarily for less. His budget would have increased outlays by $272 billion between 2010 and 2012, but investment dollars would fall by $8 billion.[9]

Promoting Socioeconomic Mobility

Socioeconomic mobility has become a very hot topic of late. Long associated with the American dream and the Horatio Alger story, socioeconomic mobility has declined over the past few decades, with the future of each generation of Americans increasingly determined by the wealth and status of their parents. To what extent does the federal budget enable socioeconomic mobility? Not just gains for those who start with lower incomes and assets, but also, more broadly, gains for anyone moving to a higher level of income?

In a study for the Pew Charitable Trust's Economic Mobility Project,[10] my coauthors and I looked at both spending and tax subsidies,[11] separating spending and tax subsidies into three categories: (1) those designed at least partly to promote mobility through subsidies for private education, saving, investment, or work; (2) those designed to boost consumption and maintain income (for example, Social Security, Medicare, cash welfare, or Supplemental Security Income), and (3) spending designed largely to promote public goods (for example, highways).[12]

A sizable slice of federal funds does go to programs that arguably try to promote mobility. In 2006, about $212 billion or 1.6 percent of GDP in direct spending, and another $534 billion or 4.1 percent of GDP in tax subsidies, went to programs at least partially designed to promote mobility. That comes to $7,000 for every household in America.[13]

Unfortunately, 72 percent of this $746 billion, or $540 billion, came mainly through programs such as tax subsidies for home ownership and other saving incentives that flow mainly to middle- and higher-income households. In absolute dollars, the subsidies rise on average as household income increases. These vehicles often provide little for lower-income households or exclude them completely. The other 28 percent came through programs that favor lower- to moderate-income individuals.

Moreover, some programs inflate key asset prices such as home prices. That puts these assets further out of reach for poor or moderate income households or young people who are just starting their careers. Thus, programs not only neglect the less well-off, they also undermine their mobility.

Unlike funds for children and investment, most of the funds for mobility fall into the general category of permanent programs that avoid the budget squeeze. Like direct spending entitlements, the largest of these subsidies (such as the tax deduction for mortgage interest to promote homeownership) are designed to grow automatically over time, regardless of changes in national priorities and needs. Yet most

Figure 6.2. *A Very Approximate Distribution of Mobility Spending Between Lower-Income and Higher-Income Households, 2006*

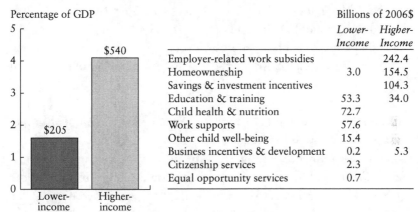

	Lower-Income	Higher-Income
Employer-related work subsidies		242.4
Homeownership	3.0	154.5
Savings & investment incentives		104.3
Education & training	53.3	34.0
Child health & nutrition	72.7	
Work supports	57.6	
Other child well-being	15.4	
Business incentives & development	0.2	5.3
Citizenship services	2.3	
Equal opportunity services	0.7	

Note: "Higher-income" includes middle-income, but the lion's share of expenditures go to households in the 4th and 5th income quintiles.

Source: Steuerle, C. Eugene, Adam Carasso, and Gillian Reynolds. 2008. "How Much Does the Federal Government Spend to Promote Economic Mobility and for Whom?" Economic Mobility Project. Washington, DC: Pew Charitable Trusts. Estimates developed using the *Budget of the United States Government FY2008,* CBO's *The Budget and Economic Outlook: Fiscal Years 2008–17,* and *Health Care Financing Review 2005.*

of this growth does not benefit poor and moderate income households and, in fact, deters their upward mobility, particularly in moving from lower- to middle-income status. Much of this subsidy goes for items like second homes of those already well off. Thus, the budget on its current path provides little and may even deter upward mobility for those who need it.

The Mismatch of Needs and Policy

Current policy suggests a very hard future ahead for programs that help children, invest in our future, and promote mobility for low- and moderate-income households. Yet these developments do not reflect the aspirations of our leaders or our people. Indeed, many of our elected officials care deeply about these programs and the problems that they seek to address. Instead, the automatic features of our budget (and much recent legislation) increasingly favors:

- end-of-life support over beginning-of-life support—that is, more support to help each person retire early and consume than to help the young build productive lives;

- consumption over investment, particularly through social welfare programs that increasingly emphasize consumption (Social Security, Medicare, and food assistance) over investment (children's education and health); and
- adequate levels of consumption for poor and moderate income households, especially for those who do not work, but exclusion from mobility-enhancing programs.

Where government fails to come through, private investment in theory could partially fill the gap, although it, too, is threatened by the economic consequences of our weak fiscal posture. But, make no mistake, while the government cannot and should not try to replace the private sector, neither can the private sector replace government. The government does too much and comprises too large of a share of our economy to avoid affecting the economy adversely as it cuts back on its investment, allocates ever larger shares of its budget to consumption, and further neglects children.

Consequence 4: Broken Government, with Antiquated Tax and Social Welfare Systems

When it comes to allocating federal resources, the issue is not solely whether more or less money supports some investment in our future. It is also whether the programs we fund are achieving their goals—meeting needs, raising living standards, and otherwise using resources well. Unfortunately, the programs that presidents and lawmakers created decades ago and that policymakers ever since have fought to maintain and expand simply are become increasingly ineffective at tackling the nation's problems. Government is not just broken; it is also antiquated.

That should not surprise us. Policymakers designed these programs for a nation and a people that have changed in ways that no one could possibly have anticipated. We are a much larger, richer, more powerful, more racially and ethnically diverse nation, with a government that has assumed far more responsibilities both at home and abroad, with an aging population and more diversified workforce, competing in an increasingly global economy whose jobs require a far higher level of education and skills than ever before. We are living longer, and in many ways better, than ever, with more access to revolutionary medical treatments and a breathtaking array of consumer comforts but with new challenges such as rising obesity. But, the programs that are increasingly coming to dominate the budget were designed for an America of yesteryear, one that is increasing passing into the history books.

That does not mean, of course, that we should simply abandon these programs due to their advancing years. Programs such as Social Security, Medicare, and Medicaid provide a certainty around which tens of millions of Americans can plan. Social Security provides an assurance for retirees that they *will* get retirement income; Medicare and Medicaid do the same for health coverage for senior citizens and the poor, respectively. The question is where to draw the line between certainty and change, between providing assurances to beneficiaries and modernizing programs so that they are affordable, target their resources well, and do not unduly drain federal resources from other important priorities.

Let us take a closer look at the "big three" federal areas in which government automatically expands according to patterns set in law largely decades ago: (1) taxes, (2) retirement, and (3) health. They bring to life the tension between certainty and change. They also highlight the problems of extraordinary inefficiency and inequity that result when applying program rules and criteria from a much earlier age to a nation and people that have evolved in dramatic, dynamic and, of course, unpredictable ways.

Taxes

Most subsidies come from tax preferences that grow automatically from year to year, whether they fulfill their purpose or not. Two of the largest, for housing and pensions, fail not only to promote mobility (as discussed above) but to fulfill their main objective of promoting saving. In fact, the government allots over $400 billion a year to promote saving for retirement, higher education, and housing, yet personal saving remains remarkably low—in some years, little more than the level of the subsidies themselves. Put another way, at least by this one measure, households use almost none of their own money to boost their savings, relying instead on government subsidies to fill their nest eggs. The numbers, and the drop in saving in recent decades (up until the Great Recession), made clear that these very expensive subsidies were not accomplishing their purposes, yet their permanent structure insured not only that they would be sustained but expanded.[14]

Why do these programs fail? For many reasons, not the least of which is that many people take advantage of the tax benefits of saving without, in fact, actually boosting their saving. For instance, they take out a second mortgage and, with more available cash, put more money into their 401(k). In doing so, they do not boost their overall saving, but they receive a tax break for their efforts. Worse, the tax benefits for ineffective saving policies drain revenues to the government, boosting deficits that will weaken the economy and, in turn, the incomes of households over the long run.

The tax system is now replete with hundreds of separate subsidies for people and businesses of almost every kind, many if not most of which generate questionable results when it comes to achieving their goals. Together, they cost the government more than $1 trillion in lost federal revenue.[15] These subsidies, also called "tax expenditures" (because they are the functional equivalent of direct spending), have received growing attention in recent years as a source of revenue both to offset the costs of cutting tax rates and to help reduce deficits. President Obama's fiscal commission and a blue-ribbon bipartisan commission of former top federal, state, and local officials recommended in late 2010 that policymakers shrink these subsidies dramatically for both of those purposes. President Reagan supported their reduction both in the deficit reduction agreements of his time as well as in the last major tax reform, the Tax Reform Act of 1986.

Taken together, some of these subsidies are just silly. Multiple subsidies for education, capital gains, housing, saving, and investment are redundant in many cases and contradictory in others. That makes the tax code more complicated, inefficient, and unfair,[16] and it also makes it harder for these subsidies to achieve their goals. Many taxpayers do not understand them or even know they are available. Meanwhile, presidents and Congresses, each determined to put its own stamp on the tax code and deliver its own new set of benefits to constituents, create more tax subsidies, as if oblivious to the fact that they're making the code harder for taxpayers even to comprehend.

This is not a book about how to create the perfect tax system. Others have tried to develop such blueprints.[17] Suffice it to say that our tax code could use a good housecleaning, with policymakers taking a close look at the hundreds of provisions to determine which ones are working well, which ones are not, and which ones either duplicate or interfere

Figure 6.3. *Expected Years of Social Security Benefits for Couples Retired at Age 65 with at Least One Partner Still Living*

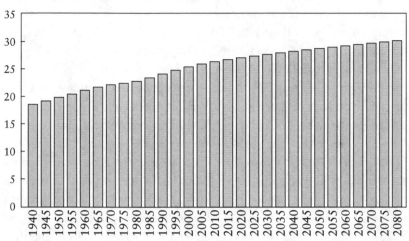

Source: Author's calculations from Social Security mortality data.

with the goals of others. Here I am focusing on government's ability to respond to changing circumstances and emerging needs, about how the growth of permanent spending or tax programs undermine the fiscal freedom of policymakers, and how tax subsidies of the kind discussed here exacerbate the problem.

Retirement

Retirement programs illustrate nicely how automatic growth features can end up concentrating additional benefits on those least likely to need them. When Social Security first paid benefits in 1940, a couple retiring at the earliest retirement age (65) would get about 18 years of benefits. Today, a couple retiring at 65 would get about 25 years' worth of benefits. Meanwhile, policymakers created an earlier retirement age of 62, even as people were living longer. For a couple born today and retiring 65 years from now, Social Security would provide more than three decades worth of benefits, and even more years if they retire as early as 62.

In essence, what began as a social insurance program for old age support has morphed into a middle-age retirement system. At this point, providing the twentieth, twenty-fifth, or thirtieth year of retirement for senior citizens has become a higher national priority than educating our kids or helping the jobless find work.

Even if affordable, smaller and smaller shares of benefits go to those who are truly "old." A few decades ago, most Social Security benefits went to those with ten years of life expectancy or less—that is, to those in the last decade of their lives. Today, only about one-third of benefits go to this older group, and close to two-thirds goes to those who are younger, with many more years of life ahead of them.

Other public retirement programs impose the same kinds of priorities on public budgets. Take state and local retirement systems, which came under great pressure as states faced budget crunches in recent years. These systems often pay benefits for many more years than even Social Security. Some recent reforms will force workers to contribute more of their pay for those benefits, but they do little to address another perverse feature of the systems: enormous penalties on workers in late middle age who want to continue working. That is because, under many of these systems, a person who works another year has to forfeit a year of retirement benefits entirely. Some teachers who are entitled to annual pensions that equal half of their annual pay effectively work at half-wages if they continue working past retirement age; for every $100 they earn, they lose $50 in pension benefits.

Or, take military pension and health benefits. Most people undoubtedly associate the defense budget with planes, tanks, and soldiers in combat. But, very high pension and health costs are consuming a larger share of the defense budget. When a person retires after twenty years of service in his or her early forties, that person and his or her spouse often can expect forty or more years of benefits. Those dollars could just as easily go to help boost the salaries of our soldiers in combat and their families or to support research—including protections against roadside bombs abroad. That they go increasingly to the pension and health benefits of retirees puts the squeeze on everything else, including the pay of our current military and our ability to respond to multiple foreign threats.

Many of these retirement programs also were designed around a stereotypical family of the 1950s—a father at work, a stay-at-home mother, and two or so children. Social Security provides a spousal and survivor benefit that would be illegal in the private sector. There, one pays for additional benefits for a wife or husband by taking a lower worker benefit. In Social Security, the worker does not pay anything extra. He or she just gets a bonus for marrying. Thus, single heads of household who raise children and pay Social Security taxes effectively contribute to spousal and survivor benefit for which they are not eligible. As a result, a working single mother who pays substantial Social Security taxes over her lifetime can receive hundreds of thousands of dollars fewer lifetime benefits than a nonworking spouse who does not raise kids or pay Social Security tax. Among those who suffer most are low-income minority women and abandoned spouses.

Or, consider divorce. In Social Security, these bonus spousal and survivor benefits are available for all those who are married to one worker for more than ten years. That means that someone who is married for nine years and eleven months and then gets divorced lacks not only access to these spousal and survivor benefits but gets no share of the worker benefits that accrues to the former spouse. By the same token, a worker who marries four times for ten years and a day each can generate four sets of spousal and survivor benefits for which he or she pays not a dime extra.

Or, consider children. In Social Security, extra benefits for children in the household are generally available to anyone receiving a benefit as a worker. This, of course, makes sense when trying to meet the needs of families with disabled workers or provide an insurance policy for survivors in case of the worker's death. But, the additional benefit also goes to workers who become eligible for retirement benefits if they still have children. That means that parents begetting children in their forties and who still support children when they are in their sixties (largely men) often get child benefits, no matter how rich they are. Such child benefits are denied to the majority of parents who have children in their twenties and thirties.

These features of Social Security would be bad enough if they continued to claim only their current level of program dollars. But these benefits are scheduled to grow larger over time as the economy grows. They reflect neither fairness nor the realities of a modern family. Policymakers should address them for reasons that stretch well beyond fiscal imbalances.[18]

Health

We have seen how open-ended government health programs enable us and our doctors to drive public health spending. In essence, Congress has abandoned its constitutional requirement to appropriate funds and has given that power to us. We can effectively borrow another dollar from China to pay for the additional health care we seek or are advised to get, at prices the doctors and hospitals and drug providers set, with providers we choose, and with procedures we agree upon. That is especially true for Medicare and, for the most part, for the tax subsidies for health care. It is less true for Medicaid to the extent that states try to control costs.

This built-in growth generates perverse health outcomes. An essentially open-ended definition of what kinds of treatments qualify for federal health care dollars nourishes additional growth in health care services that does not relate costs closely with benefits.

Consider the following examples of distortions in our health delivery system:

- *Chronic care over cures.* One health care executive told me privately that his company worked much more on drugs for chronic care, for which the company would receive reimbursements for years, than on cures, for which the company might receive a one-time payment from each consumer.

- *Acute care over prevention.* Many preventive efforts are not eligible for federal subsidies. Little is available, for instance, for public health campaigns to deter obesity—even though we will have to spend far more public dollars on the health care problems that obesity creates.

- *Elderly health care over child health care.* Children have access to the lowest-cost doctors (pediatricians and general practitioners) while the elderly, who use far more health care than children, have much more access to surgeons who often earn two or even three times as much, yet on a preventative basis may provide much less lifetime benefit to their patients.

Health is our only major growth industry in which we see a large growth in prices at the same time as growth in the amount of services provided.[19] Consider computers, telecommunications, and even recreation. In those industries, growth encourages much more competition among providers, ensuring that prices in those industries either fall or grow more slowly than prices in general.

The health reform law that President Obama and Congress enacted in 2010 includes numerous provisions to encourage health care efficiencies. The Congressional Budget Office, however, concluded that they had only a modest chance of "bending the health cost curve"—that is, simply slowing its inexorable rate of growth. Without serious budget constraints, providers have little reason to become more efficient even when research reveals new ways to do so. If the money is flowing freely, why reduce the number of doctors who visit patients? Why try to invent cures for disease when you can make more by treating chronic problems with drugs year after year?

I served for several years on the National Committee for Vital and Health Statistics, which spearheaded efforts to enable hospitals and doctors to adopt electronic health records. Such records insure that, when people get sick in strange places, new doctors can quickly find their medical histories. Such records prevent duplicative efforts and help pharmacists more easily discover when doctors acting independently prescribe to an individual multiple drugs that contravene each other. Perhaps more promisingly, electronic health records can provide a base of information for detecting disease early on and potentially discovering common causes for some problems, such as autism, for which we know too little. But hospitals and doctors simply had no incentive to adopt such a procedure because their payments were not based on the quality of outcomes or even of outputs like an electronic health record. The federal government recently spent tens of billions of dollars to encourage the use of such records, but it has made little adjustment in payment rates according to the quality of care provided. The open-ended nature of the health budget almost insures that electronic health records will fail to save on cost as well, since the new information will likely generate more rather than fewer referrals for health services.[20]

To be sure, a wide range of programs—from welfare to transportation to rental housing subsidies—suffer from well-known problems, inequities, and inefficiencies. With programs that do not grow automatically, and especially with programs that are funded through annual appropriations, policymakers can simply let these programs shrink or even die. When they do grow automatically, however, the problems with these programs, and their lack of accommodation to new economic demands and possibilities, grow in importance each year as program budgets increase. Built-in growth creates ever-more promises that policymakers must make an affirmative effort to rescind, rather than just allow to wither away. It is this type of political consequence to which we turn next.

7

The Three Deadly
Political Consequences

When the Athenians finally wanted not to give to society but for society to give to them, when the freedom they wished for most was freedom from responsibility, then Athens ceased to be free.

—Edward Gibbon
The Decline and Fall of the Roman Empire

Along with four deadly economic consequences, our fiscal foolishness nourishes three deadly political consequences that go a long way to explain why policymakers find it so hard to address the problem at hand and why today's politics are so partisan.

The three political consequences—three difficult and interrelated political dilemmas—are unique to our time: (1) the decline of "fiscal democracy," as previous decisions by dead and retired policymakers deprive today's and future generations of the power to make their own decisions; (2) a classic "prisoners' dilemma," in which liberals and conservatives alike assess correctly that they will "lose" politically by acquiescing to spending cuts or tax increases, respectively, to reduce budget deficits or create budget flexibility; and (3) obstacles to "fixing" government because, to address new priorities or create new programs, elected officials must renege on old promises, telling people they are no longer entitled to the higher benefits or low taxes that they have come to expect.

These three political consequences reinforce one another, leaving us in a kind of governmental paralysis. Fiscal democracy shrinks, the prisoners' dilemma deters steps to address it, and other obstacles to fixing government reduce fiscal democracy even more. The less fiscal freedom, the more difficult is the task of restoring it, making it ever harder for the younger generations of today and tomorrow to create a government that can address the unique challenges that they will face.

Consequence 1: The Decline in Fiscal Democracy

More than any other age group, young people have the right to be unhappy with the government they have inherited.

Let us return to our basic figure on fiscal democracy (Figure 1.1), introduced in the first chapter. Federal programs that are already in place will eventually claim all federal revenues, as they did in 2009—and continue to claim them for fifty, one hundred, and two hundred years from now. Even a substantial growth in revenues will not remove this straightjacket, except temporarily, because automatic spending (which includes not just spending but also tax deductions, credits, and other write-offs in the tax code that grow automatically) is scheduled to grow continually faster than the economy.

Now, compare the fiscal freedom that older generations of voters enjoyed with that of the generations of today and tomorrow. Older generations may not always have chosen well, but they had much more flexibility to create the government they wanted. They chose, for instance, to create the social welfare expansions of the 1960s and 1970s. They chose to create health and retirement programs for themselves that grew faster than the economy and for whose benefits they often did not pay. They chose to keep their tax rates below the levels necessary to finance the government they had erected, especially with the tax cuts of the early 1980s and early 2000s. To their credit, they expanded the social welfare state to meet needs for which they, as individuals, may not have benefited, and they avoided the temptations of more onerous socialistic systems that proponents widely advocated and that many European nations widely adopted at the beginning and middle of the twentieth century.[1]

Liberals and conservatives alike congratulate themselves on what they have accomplished, and they assume that younger generations will thank them for their efforts.

Liberals expect the young to fight to maintain the spending programs that they have built. If anything, they expect young people to expand those programs further, and they bitterly fight those who would stand in their way. They are blind to the reality of built-in spending and tax subsidy trends—to the fact that existing programs will already absorb not only future revenues that the current tax system will generate, but eventually all of the revenues that almost any tax increase would generate.

Conservatives expect the young to fight to keep tax rates low—implying, but seldom saying, that to do so while maintaining all the automatically growing spending programs and tax subsidies would require drastic cuts in all of the programs that are designed to serve the young, as well as most of those serving middle-aged working Americans. They ignore the extent to which tax cuts that are financed by deficits really are not tax cuts at all, but simply transfers of burdens to future taxpayers. They, too, expect the young to thank them for keeping government out of their lives—except, of course, that many conservatives also tell us that government should keep its hands off of growing Medicare benefits whenever Democrats even begin to lean in that direction.

Today, liberals and conservatives no longer spend much time examining broader goals of government or broader principles behind their actions. At best, they might agree on the need to reduce government debt to sustainable levels. But, have you heard many liberals discuss how much is enough—for instance, whether government should finance a twenty-fifth year of a couple's retirement, or why it should give future retired couples $1.5 million of lifetime old age benefits in retirement as opposed to the about $1 million for newly retired couples today? Have you heard many conservatives admit that spending that is hidden in the tax code in the form of deductions, credits, and other write-offs is a form of larger government or acknowledge how tax cuts financed by the bonds that we sell to China and oil-producing states put our economic destiny increasingly in the hands of authoritarian leaders who do not share our interests?

Fighting to protect their past legislative achievements, both sides now expect the young to work more to pay off more debt owed to more foreigners—and with little expectation to date that policymakers will reverse that situation. Even the most daring of policymakers who are willing to address our budget challenges tend to be timid in their approach. Liberals and conservatives alike claim that in reforming Social Security, they should ask nothing of those who have already reached the age of 55—that is, nothing from that third of the population that controls half of the nation's wealth and is scheduled over the next twenty years to get almost all the benefits from the automatic expansion of existing programs. The less that this older generation contributes to restore some measure of fiscal sanity, the more that others will have to pay—in this case, the "others" will largely be younger generations, including those not yet born. What today are called minorities will also together comprise the new majority of those left to pay the bills.

Think of it this way: liberals and conservatives alike want the young to protect the monuments they have erected, even if those monuments now sit in both lanes of traffic, preventing the young from driving on either side of the street.

The Real Victims

But let us set aside for the moment our calculus of winners and losers, of who gets what and who pays what. It is at the ballot box where the decline in fiscal democracy comes most clearly to light. The issue is not merely the economic and political inefficiency of dead and retired policymakers with limited knowledge of the future trying to foreordain the future of government. It is the effort of those prior policymakers to deny their successors the freedom to choose.

Together, the combination of programs that grow forever and taxes that are inadequate to finance them creates an imbalance in the political rights of different generations. In essence, we treat future generations as adolescents who cannot make decisions for themselves.

Liberals and conservatives who are largely wed to these twentieth-century fights, of course, claim to be in very different camps. But, in this sense, they are really in cahoots with one another in trying to ensure their hold over the government of the future—defined, of course, as a government devoted to priorities that previous policymakers had set.

Like all "isms," the liberalism and conservatism of any period are defined as much by the period as by any consistent set of principles. The liberalism and conservatism of 1965, for instance, only partially resembled those of 1900. So why should social welfare expansion of the 1960s and early 1970s or low taxes that are rooted in the tax cuts of 1981 and 2001 define priorities for 2015 or 2030? Will future liberals really believe that a top government priority is to grant a typical couple about three decades of retirement support? Will future conservatives really believe that deficit-raising tax cuts are free lunches rather than burdens left to future taxpayers?

Disputes over priorities are not new. What's new is that they formerly played out mainly in battles over *current* spending and taxes, leaving future levels of spending and taxes largely for future generations to decide. The fiscal freedom with which early generations made those decisions was created by revenues that were rising faster than commitments. Policymakers could expand government as a share of the economy, but they did not have to do so in order to finance their previous commitments. It was a choice, not a necessity.

The young generation of today and those to come will no longer have that choice. The growing revenues of their days are already committed—and, in many countries, more than fully committed. Just to finance the commitments of dead or retired policymakers, they will have to raise their own average tax rates ever higher—and, eventually, even that will not solve the problem. Their only alternative is to try to deny to others—largely, older generations who are growing in number and, thus, will have even more political power—the benefits to which they feel entitled.

To be clear, this is not a suggestion that we should end all stable or permanent programs. It is merely the suggestion that when the fiscal democracy index approaches zero or falls below it for future years, we have gone way too far in creating programs that grow automatically and increasingly dominate our budget. We have gone way too far in building in increases and tax cuts that will be financed by future deficits, thus shifting the burden of paying the costs to future voters.

We have focused mainly on the United States here, yet factors driving the growth in the share of national income devoted to government retirement and health care and tax subsidy programs are quite common across national lines.[2] Regardless of when or whether each country hits a "tipping point," more built-in promises and more attempts to preordain future rather than current budgets reduce fiscal democracy.

Consequence 2: The Prisoners' Dilemma

In the classic prisoners' dilemma, the police arrest two people for a crime and then separate them from one another for questioning. (Let us presume for the moment that they did, in fact, commit the crime.) Each must decide whether to keep quiet or "rat" on the other. If each stays quiet, each gets only a minor penalty, because the cops lack the evidence to justify something harsher. But, if the first rats out the second, while the second stays quiet, or vice versa, then the one who rats goes free while the other gets a harsh penalty. If they both rat on each other, they both get harsher penalties than if they both stayed quiet.

Acting alone, either suspect would seem to gain by betraying the other. In the classic set-up, suppose the first prisoner rats. The second should do likewise to get a less-harsh penalty. If, instead, the first prisoner stays quiet, the second can go free by betraying the first. So, it always seems better to betray the other even though, together, they both will get harsher penalties than if they both stayed quiet.

Our budget mess closely resembles this classic prisoners' dilemma.

When the game shifted from a traditional debate over controlling the present to trying to control the future, it made sense for liberals and conservatives, acting independently, to control it as best they could before the other one did. That way, they could remove the power of the other party to reverse course even in the future.

Now that both parties have imposed their agendas on the future, the challenge is no longer to stop them from doing so. The challenge, instead, is how to convince each to give up some of that control and, thus, restore fiscal freedom for future generations. Both parties would gain more by restoring greater balance and flexibility, but each mistrusts the other to do the same and stick with it. In public, each party rats out the other—that is, each blames the other pre-emptively (liberals blame conservatives for wanting to destroy Social Security and Medicare, conservatives blame liberals for wanting to raise taxes to ever-higher levels).

What neither is willing to do, unfortunately, is precisely what we need them to do—to come clean, together, with the American people about the problem at hand, and to work with one another to restore flexibility to the budget. They can't even take care of the first deadly economic consequence: engaging in enough spending cuts and tax increases to achieve stability or a sustainable path for future debt, much less the discretion to change course. Both fear the political consequences of doing so.

How the Prisoners' Dilemma Plays Out

Consider both parties' view of recent fiscal history:

- Democrats believe that they lost control of Congress in the 1994 mid-term elections because they worked with President Clinton in 1993 to raise taxes as part of an effort to reduce deficits.

- Democrats believe that former Vice President Walter Mondale lost the 1984 presidential election as soon as he said that he would raise taxes.
- Republicans believe that George H. W. Bush lost his presidential re-election bid in 1992 because, contrary to his dramatic "read my lips" promise, he agreed to raise taxes in 1990 as part of an effort to reduce deficits.
- Republicans believe that they lost control of the Senate in the 1986 mid-term elections because, a year earlier, they had proposed a broad plan to reduce the deficits that included a freeze on Social Security benefits.

These time-worn views reinforce the prisoners' dilemma.

These party views may be somewhat simplistic, but they contain elements of truth. The party that separately tries to move the budget toward balance often loses out.[3] Jude Wanniski was not entirely wrong when he warned Republicans that they needed to be Santa Claus, too, since their budget-balancing efforts would merely give Democrats greater flexibility to spend more later.[4] Democrats were not entirely wrong to believe that their budget-balancing of the 1990s gave George W. Bush the leeway to cut taxes deeply in the early 2000s.

What about the American people? After decades of expanding retirement and health and tax subsidy programs that grow automatically, providing ever-higher levels of benefits to tens of millions of Americans, have we come to feel entitled to it all? Have we come to expect that we will live a third of our adult lives in retirement that is financed by someone else? Have we come to expect low tax rates and generous write-offs for employer-provided health care and home mortgage interest and savings and investment? If we are business people, have we come to believe that all of our tax breaks are sacrosanct, even those that leave some business people with lower marginal tax rates than average citizens and some businesses with negative tax rates on new investment financed with borrowed dollars?

To a great extent, we have. Polls indicate that we express little inclination to accept less from Social Security and Medicare or to pay higher taxes (though some of the non-rich are more than happy to see the rich pay more, and some who do not receive welfare benefits are more than happy to cut welfare programs). Worse, we express ourselves not just as average Americans, but also as members of defined groups, whether that is as senior citizens, health care consumers, homeowners, veterans, or others.

Consider how this dynamic plays out in the corridors of power in Washington. Suppose, for purposes of fiscal responsibility, a lawmaker were to oppose a bill that would not only reward our armed forces in recent combat but also provide extra benefits to veterans far removed from combat—extra benefits, that is, that are harder to justify. The powerful veterans' groups, with their Washington offices, would quickly mount a public campaign to pressure that lawmaker to change his or her mind. They would urge their members to write to the lawmaker, send him e-mails, and call his office. They would write op-ed columns in the lawmaker's local newspapers and air television and radio advertisements in his district. Meanwhile, no one would mount a vigorous campaign to defend the lawmaker on the basis of fiscal responsibility. Few would call his office, and no one would air advertisements on his behalf.

None of this is new, of course. Policymakers have been struggling with this reality in Washington for decades. *The Triumph of Politics,*[5] the gripping, behind-the-scenes account of President Reagan's budget director, David Stockman, to convince his own administration colleagues and lawmakers of both parties to cut the deficit, remains a classic. Numerous White House officials and members of Congress have since written their own accounts of the political landmines that stand in the way of responsible fiscal policymaking.

Nor are things different on the tax side. As part of a landmark tax reform plan, the Treasury Department proposed in 1984 to eliminate tax preferences that favored richer veterans over poorer ones. Those tax breaks did little or nothing for low- or moderate-income veterans with low or zero income tax rates because the size of one's tax break was directly related to that veteran's income and tax rate. Under the proposal, tax breaks would go more evenly to veterans based on need, and they would no longer favor veterans with high-paying jobs or rich spouses over veterans with neither. In response, veterans' groups indicated that, if the department kept that provision in its tax reform plan, they would air an advertisement in which a Treasury official would ask a paraplegic veteran, "And just why do you think you deserve a tax break?" Needless to say, the department dropped that provision.[6]

But, it gets worse. Lawmakers face pressure not just from those of the other party, and not just from senior citizens, veterans, and other private interests. They face pressure from within their own political circles.

On the Republican side, the private "Club for Growth" attacks moderate Republicans who sometimes express interest in raising taxes, and the group supports conservative alternatives to them in party primaries. At Americans for Tax Reform, President Grover Norquist seeks to convince candidates of both parties to sign a "no new taxes" pledge, and he serves as an enforcer when Republicans, in particular, suggest that they may violate their own signed pledge and raise taxes. Ronald Reagan, who remains a conservative icon, would be ostracized from today's Republican Party for the many tax increases that he signed into law after 1981. On the Democratic side, liberal groups serve as the functional equivalents of the "Club for Growth" and Americans for Tax Reform as they pressure Democrats to oppose any changes in Social Security and Medicare.[7]

On Capitol Hill, the parties reinforce the ideological purity that the outside groups demand. In the House, leaders of both parties have centralized their control over committee assignments and campaign support. They allocate desirable committee slots to those who support their party's hard-core ideological agenda and deny them to those who express more flexibility.

Consider the failures of both the Republican "starve the beast" strategy and the Democratic "feed the beast" strategy. Under "starve the beast," following tax cuts, policymakers would eventually cut spending programs if the revenues were not there to support them. Reagan was among the champions of this view, saying of Washington pols, "We can lecture our children about extravagance until we run out of voice and breath. Or we can cure their extravagance simply by reducing their allowance."[8]

But, Bruce Bartlett, an original architect of Reagan's big 1981 tax cuts, notes that, under George W. Bush, another small government proponent, spending as a share of the economy boomed even as revenues fell.[9] Like many, Bartlett concludes "not only that the theory doesn't work at all, but is in fact perverse."[10]

Meanwhile, as Wanniski described it, Democrats effectively employed a "feed the beast" strategy—enacting spending increases that prompted tax increases to cover the costs. As with "starve the beast," the extent to which that theory reflects our recent fiscal experience is open to question.[11]

Both starving and feeding, however, were far more relevant under earlier circumstances. When discretionary spending dominated the budget and policymakers pursued budget balancing, a tax cut indeed would likely prompt lower spending, while higher spending would likely prompt higher taxes. With wider acceptance of deficit spending and the growth in "mandatory" spending, policymakers no longer follow a giveaway in the form of a tax cut or spending increase with budget-balancing efforts.[12]

Today, neither Democrats nor Republicans would be wrong to claim that their side's efforts at deficit reduction only give the other side more leeway later to pursue tax cuts or spending increases. Both parties emerged from this multi-decade post-war fiscal history suspicious of the other. Neither believes that it can succeed politically or economically by taking the lead on deficit-cutting efforts. The onus of 1990 and 1993 budget agreements still hangs over them: they view takeaways as the path to political suicide.

Consequence 3: Obstacles to Fixing Government

Our elected officials come to Washington to "do" things—to strengthen national defense, improve education, expand access to health care, and so on. Liberal or conservative, a president or member of Congress arrives in the nation's capital with an agenda. Even during times of peace and prosperity, even during times of broad public satisfaction, the nation faces challenges at home and abroad. Our elected leaders and their staffs focus on their own particular areas of interest and, in those areas, try to use the power of government to address the problems at hand.

At this stage, however, the nation's leaders feel increasingly boxed in, unable to steer new federal resources (in the form of more spending or tax cuts) to new priorities. With health and retirement programs already claiming the additional revenues that a growing economy will gener-ate in the years ahead, elected officials will be hard-pressed to find the resources to finance their priorities. The only way to find resources for new priorities is to renege on old promises—to tell senior citizens that they cannot have all the health and retirement benefits that they were expecting, or to tell taxpayers that their tax subsidies are not sacrosanct and they cannot expect today's tax rates to stay as low as they are now.

Growing deficits only exacerbate the problem. Since those deficits are economically unsustainable, as we have noted, we will have to reduce them. At some point, our lenders will force us to do so because they simply will not lend us the money to finance them. That means that our elected leaders already have to take more away from people (in the form of tax increases or spending cuts) than they can give them (in the form of tax cuts or spending increases). The longer we wait and allow long-term deficits and debt to grow even after the economy has recovered, the more we will have to raise taxes and cut spending just to cover the higher interest costs. So, they will have to take benefits away from people to avoid economic calamity, but still without giving them anything tangible in return.

Shrinking fiscal freedom threatens political stability. The public demonstrations that stretched from Athens, Greece, to Madison, Wisconsin, may be a sign of more to come. In no small part, these battles involve not just current resources but the hoped-for revenues that a growing economy will generate. Consequently, any effort to reduce deficits to sustainable levels under policies largely or completely set by dead and retired legislators will not end these battles. Only by more broadly rescinding promises for ever-growing benefits and low taxes can we restore fiscal freedom. People will then fight mainly over new directions for government, not on the denial of benefits to which they feel entitled or have become accustomed.

All of this represents a new form of political agony for the democratic process. Never before in American history have elected officials faced the challenge that steering government in fundamentally new directions requires reneging on the fundamental promises of their predecessors. That is why officials largely refuse to level with their constituents about the problem at hand. They pretend that we just need to tinker around the edges of government, reduce "waste, fraud, and abuse," cut the salaries and benefits of federal employees, stop sending aid to other countries, or stop helping the undeserving poor. They largely refuse to acknowledge that the problem is more basic, that it derives from excessive promises that claim all of the revenues that even a fast-growing economy can hope to generate and from the corresponding promise to refuse to collect enough revenues to pay our bills.

Where Does That Leave Us?

To be sure, we expect more from our elected leaders. We expect them to, well, *lead*. But both we and the leaders who want to restore fiscal sanity and create a more appropriate government for the twenty-first century must recognize the obstacles that stand in the way. For starters, as described above, policymakers have learned some hard lessons from the past quarter-century. They have learned that, among voters, they make few friends and create many enemies by telling the truth and trying to address our fiscal problems. They learn that, when it comes to fiscal policy, inaction is safer than action.[13]

Making matters worse, issues like Social Security, health care, and taxation are extremely complicated. It is essentially impossible to have a reasonable debate about policy options in the context of a political campaign. The issues are too easy to demagogue.

Our leaders also face a changing political landscape that reinforces the "classic prisoners' dilemma" and further incentivizes inaction. As political parties have weakened in recent decades, private groups have stepped up to perform some of their functions. For their campaigns, incumbents and candidates raise money and secure the ground troops from private groups. For Democrats, they come from labor unions and their liberal allies; for Republicans, from chambers of commerce and other associations that represent business. Dependent on outside groups for their political futures, they are disinclined to anger them later by reneging on the promises of higher benefits and low taxes that these private interests have come to expect.

Moreover, state legislatures have increasingly redrawn congressional districts so that they overwhelmingly include Democratic voters or Republican voters rather than more of a 50-50 mix. Once in office, the lawmakers who represent those districts are, thus, more inclined to defend the one-party agendas of their district majorities than seek bipartisan solutions to problems. On the fiscal front, that means that we increasingly have a Congress of Democrats who will defend all existing pillars of the social welfare state and of Republicans who will threaten to shut down the government rather than raise taxes or even pay bondholders for the debt they created. That dynamic presents another major hurdle to the goal of restoring fiscal freedom.[14]

Not surprisingly, Congress is increasingly dominated by hard-core liberals on the left and hard-core conservatives on the right. Moderates of the middle—who were inclined to eschew dogmatism, work across party lines, and compromise with one another to reach public policy goals—are shrinking in number and declining in influence. In the 2012 election, moderate Democratic senators Joseph Lieberman of Connecticut, Ben Nelson of Nebraska, Kent Conrad of North Dakota, and Jeff Bingaman of New Mexico, along with Republican senators Olympia Snowe of Maine and Kay Bailey Hutchinson of Texas, all decided not to run for reelection. Several of them, along with several moderate House members who announced their retirements, said they were tired of the growing polarization in Washington and the reduced chances of bipartisan cooperation.

Despite widespread views to the contrary, today's lawmakers are not ethically or morally inferior to their predecessors. In fact, due to campaign finance laws and ethics rules, they are probably cleaner and more honest than ever. Their ferocity probably pales in comparison to the lawmakers of our antebellum period, and they engage in far fewer conflicts of interest between their professional responsibilities and their personal gain than lawmakers of the Gilded Age. On the fiscal front, however, today's lawmakers face a series of political obstacles that largely prevent them from restoring the fiscal freedom that both they and their successors desperately need if they hope to create a government for tomorrow.

Restoring fiscal freedom may not be sufficient to create or restore greater bipartisanship, but it is necessary to remove each of the three political dilemmas and make working across party lines less costly for those who do it.

8

The Counter-Revolution

The stultifying demands for an unreasonable level of predictive certainty are not the monopoly of any political group. While political conservatives usually "insist on an absolute concept of national security," political liberals tend to "insist on an absolute security with respect to safety, health, and environmental problems. . . ." Both have smuggled Darwinian expectations, axioms borrowed from the animal and vegetable kingdoms, into our new machine kingdom. Both demand insurance against unimagined progress. Both discourage us from a quest for the peculiar vagrancy of our new world, from a search for the laws of the unexpected.

—Daniel J. Boorstin,
Cleopatra's Nose: Essays on the Unexpected[1]

A decade into a new century, we have remarkable opportunities to create a brighter, healthier, and more prosperous future for our nation and its people. But, we are stuck in place, unable to take full advantage of these opportunities because we lack the fiscal freedom to shift direction, make choices, and set new priorities. Unable to let go of our policy past, we cannot shape our future.

It took us several decades to get to this point, as policymakers created and expanded permanent retirement, health, tax, and other subsidy programs that grow automatically from year to year, while locking in tax rates too low to finance the government we had built. When it comes to restoring fiscal freedom, our challenge is enormous—and growing by the day. As in previous fiscal turnings, what took decades to create, may in turn take years, perhaps decades, to address.

Nor should we expect the apologists for the status quo to sit quietly and watch others challenge the policy monuments that they created and have so vociferously defended ever since. Indeed, we should expect the forces of the status quo to mount a counter-revolution, to dig in their heels and oppose all efforts to rethink the promises of yesterday and their implications for tomorrow. Their arguments will likely fall into three main categories:

- We should focus on the ever-present battle over size of government above all else.
- We must always increase, and never reduce, the economic security and certainty that government promises to the American people.
- We can always reform and make hard choices later; even if they drive to the cliff of some disaster, policymakers inevitably will prevent us from falling over it.

The best of their arguments have some basis. In the end, however, they fail to mitigate the challenge at hand. They merely suggest that policymakers act with balance and good judgment.

Big, Small, or Working Government

Few politicians of either party argue for bigger government these days. Though Republicans typically claim the small government mantra, Democrats have been recognizing limits as well. In his 2009 inaugural address, President Obama said that "[t]he question we ask today is not whether our government is too big or too small, but whether it works." In a sense, Obama was echoing President Clinton's efforts to "reinvent" government, a central focus of Vice President Al Gore's tenure as Clinton's White House partner. He also was echoing Clinton's oft-cited line from his 1996 State of the Union address: "the era of big government is over." [2]

Of course, rhetoric and reality do not always match one another. In terms of growth in domestic policy spending throughout our history, modern Republican Presidents clearly dominate (again, see the Appendix).

In the 1990s, pundits suggested that Clinton was claiming small-government conservatism for himself. In fact, he was trying to position himself in the same place as Obama—in the political center. For, after stating that "the era of big government is over," Clinton went on to say, "But we cannot go back to the time when our citizens were left to fend for themselves. Instead, we must go forward. . . . Self-reliance and teamwork are not opposing virtues; we must have both."

Clinton and Obama may have issued their pronouncements for political purposes but, in many ways, it does not matter. Arithmetic drives one to the same conclusion. Short on resources and devoid of fiscal freedom, elected officials must make government "work" better—make it more efficient, enable it to meet its tasks without depending upon ever-larger shares of national income. That would allow them to do new things by relying more on the additional revenue that a growing economy will generate. By contrast, efforts to leave existing programs alone, to defend the status quo out of fears of what might come next, will continue to deter progress and leave us with an antiquated government.

For the past half-century, federal revenues have averaged 18.5 percent of our GDP and spending has averaged closer to 20 percent. Presidents and Congresses have seesawed back and forth for at least the last quarter-century on whether to set the top income tax rate facing only a small share of taxpayers at 28 percent or 35 percent or 40 percent—as if that issue defined whether government worked. Spending far too much time on that issue, our leaders spent far too little on whether the tax system as a whole, as well as our educational, social welfare, and pension and health systems, served us well.

Looking at the Past, and the Future

Let us compare the period since 1930—which has brought a huge growth in government as a share of GDP—with some future date by which our government could grow to the higher average level among developed economies (mainly Western Europe) or perhaps shrink by an equivalent amount.

In 1930, federal spending was about 3.5 percent of GDP. Now, let us presume that government remained at about that level in the ensuing decades. The income of Americans has expanded about six-fold since then, making possible a six-fold increase in government spending, even at 3.5 percent of GDP. But, of course, that is not what happened. Since 1930, federal spending as a share of GDP expanded an additional six-fold—from about 3.5 percent to more than 20 percent today. A six-fold increase in income multiplied by a six-fold increase in spending out of that income meant about a thirty-six-fold increase in total real spending.

Looking forward, the debate in Washington is not over whether to boost the rate of spending another six-fold (so that it grows from 20-plus percent to over 120 percent of GDP). Instead, it is whether to emulate higher Western European levels of government spending for which average spending of all levels of government combined is about six percentage points of GDP higher than in the United States, stop somewhere between our current level and theirs, stay where we are, or drop a few percentage points.

For some liberals, Western Europe is the ideal for social policy; for some conservatives, it is the worst possible outcome. Either way, the math is unmistakable for both Western Europe and ourselves: we cannot sustain the automatic growth in spending simply by deciding that we will let government grow unimpeded as a share of the economy.

But how much does all this debate over European or U.S. levels of government matter? More than ever, most new resources that government will spend will depend on economic growth—regardless of whether government's share of the economy rises or falls by a few percentage points.

Figures 8.1 and 8.2 compare the rise in spending that economic growth makes possible to the rise in spending that is generated by an explicit decision to expand the scope of government—both historically and under a presumed jump by about six percentage points of GDP. As the figures make clear, to make government "work," policymakers' primary task is to decide how to best use the additional revenues that normal economic growth generates. A six-percentage-point increase in the share of GDP translates to less than a 30 percent growth in the real efforts of government, as opposed to the more than 500 percent growth that occurred because of government's expanded share of the economic pie since 1930. The growth in government efforts potentially generated by economic growth, on the other hand, remains as unbounded in the future as the past.

Indeed, the figures understate the huge role that economic growth will play in generating revenues—and the huge stakes in developing appropriate tax and spending policies. Those policies can either support future growth or undermine it, whereas the figures simply assume some normalcy with the past. Recent sovereign debt crises in many European

Figure 8.1. *Real Per Capita Government Spending, Under Various Scenarios, Historical*

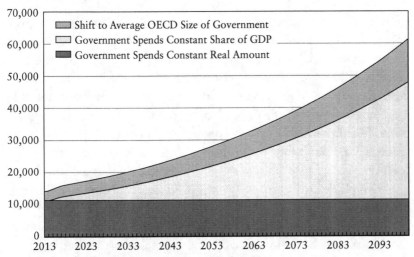

14,000

- ▨ Actual Spending
- ☐ Government Spends Constant Share of GDP
- ▨ Government Spends Constant Real Amount

12,000

10,000

8,000

6,000

4,000

2,000

0

1940   1950   1960   1970   1980   1990   2000   2010

Source: Author's calculations from OMB Historical Tables and Census data. Values are in constant 2013 dollars. "Constant Real Amount" keeps federal spending per capita fixed at its 1940 level, adjusted for inflation. "Constant Share of GDP" shows total federal spending as a share of GDP remaining at its 1940 level, about 9.8 percent of GDP.

Figure 8.2. *Real Per Capita Government Spending, Under Various Scenarios, Projected*

70,000

- ▨ Shift to Average OECD Size of Government
- ☐ Government Spends Constant Share of GDP
- ▨ Government Spends Constant Real Amount

60,000

50,000

40,000

30,000

20,000

10,000

0

2013   2023   2033   2043   2053   2063   2073   2083   2093

Source: Author's calculations based on CBO and Census projections. "Constant Real Amount" fixes federal spending per capita at its 2012 level, adjusted for inflation. "Constant Share of GDP" keeps total federal spending fixed at 21.5 percent of GDP. "Shift to OECD Size" assumes total federal spending rises to 27.5 percent of GDP (a 6 percentage-point increase) and remains at that level.

countries here at the beginning of the twenty-first century only reinforce the point.

Economic Security and Certainty

Does government have a legitimate role to play in promoting the economic security and certainty of the American people? Of course. Many of the successes of twentieth-century government reflected its efforts to do so. In many ways, government dramatically reduced poverty and improved the health of many Americans. But, in some ways, government has moved far beyond its original mandate. It now supports retirement in late middle age, not just old age. It spends a lot of its health care dollars raising the incomes of health providers (doctors, insurance companies, and so on) rather than helping health care consumers. It supports rich farmers according to formulas developed for poor farmers of a different era. In these and many other cases, it fails to use public money resourcefully; for many programs, it barely keeps track of who benefits, by how much, and how efficiently it is meeting its goals. Many forms of spending and tax subsidies grow eternally, even as the government fails to direct them to solve something and without regard to new, higher priority goals that might come along.

Both conservatives and liberals have drawn inappropriate conclusions from government's record. On the right, some critics have moved beyond legitimate conservative concerns about waste and disincentives to work and save to attack the basic concept of progressivity—that those with the most resources must pay more and those with the greatest needs should benefit more. Other critics suggest that government should have only a very limited role in ensuring economic security for anyone. At the libertarian Cato Institute, one senior fellow said the federal government "shouldn't have any role in the field of income distribution."[3] Such criticisms, however, do not withstand even cursory scrutiny.

Should all members of a family—including its youngest children—contribute equally to the family's survival and upkeep? Of course not. If, then, conservatives accept that parents and perhaps older children should assume the entire or overwhelming share of the burden, then they believe in some level of progressivity and redistribution. When, moreover, they argue that government should confine domestic spending more to the poor (rather than provide cradle-to-grave insurance for the broad middle class), they apply to government spending the same principle of progressivity that they just denied.

Since at least the days of Adam Smith, conservatives and liberals alike have generally recognized that the rich can much more easily support government functions than others and, consequently, they should. Simply as a practical matter, how much tax can government collect from someone with no income?

On the left, liberals often pay inadequate attention to goals other than progressivity. Good intentions are not enough to create good programs. When government cannot run programs well, they generate corruption and, more broadly, public cynicism toward government. Practical matters of implementation matter. Government officials, elected or otherwise, act as agents for themselves, not just the society they are supposed to serve and, therefore, they must be constrained in the power they exercise.

Moreover, incentives matter. Taxes can discourage work and saving. They almost always produce unintended and unwanted costs and consequences, such as corporations that claim new headquarters abroad, people who refuse to sell assets simply to avoid tax, and households that consume fewer taxed goods and services and more untaxed ones.

Providing Economic Security

Currently, much if not most government spending and regulation is designed to provide some measure of economic security and certainty. Those are surely noble goals. Problems arise, however, when those goals crowd out others, when they demand too much of the potential governmental pie, and when the demands for public resources to satisfy those goals leave us without the resources to address other goals. At that point, we should reconsider our assumptions, recalibrate the tax and spending formulas that are embedded in these programs, and rebalance old priorities with new ones.[4]

Take, for instance, the issue of how to boost economic security by reducing risk. When it comes to investing in the private sector, experts advise that individuals diversify their investments. An individual should buy a variety of stocks and mutual funds so that he or she does not lose everything if one particular stock or other asset crashes. That is a diversifiable or avoidable risk.

The same applies to government. The government can help diversify some risks, but often merely shifts risks from one group to another, thus providing security to some groups by taking it from others. In some other cases, government programs actually increase risks.

Consider what occurred in the years leading up to the Great Recession. When government provided excessive guarantees for unduly risky financial loans, many banks and other financial institutions were more than happy to play the game of, "Heads I win, tails you lose." If they made the loan or if borrowers made their payments on their loans, financial managers garnered huge bonuses. If borrowers defaulted, government—that is, other taxpayers—was left holding the bag.

Or, consider the government's recent experience with pension insurance under the Pension Benefit Guarantee Corporation. As designed, the insurance did not just diversity risks, but also offered special subsidized protections to plans that inadequately funded the benefits they promised. However, the government charged premiums to all pension plans, adequately funded or otherwise. Some firms increased their risks or avoided them simply by shifting risks to other firms or taxpayers. In essence, the government unfairly distributed its pension insurance—shifting costs from old to young, from men to women who were less likely to garner the insurance payments, and from one set of workers and firms to others—sometimes increasing overall risks.

So, government does have a role to play in providing economic security by reducing risks. But, it must distinguish between reducing risks and merely shifting them to others or, worse, increasing them for the population as a whole. When it makes excessive promises for the future—promises that it almost certainly cannot fulfill—government adds to societal risks ranging from sovereign debt crises, to weakened ability to respond to recessions, to increased default risks by organizations benefitting from guarantees, to new and unexpected tax burdens for both businesses and households.

Providing Economic Certainty

Next, let us take the closely related issue of providing certainty. As an example, retirees who are collecting Social Security, or something like it, legitimately need some certainty that they can collect their benefits and that those benefits will not fall as they grow older, more feeble, and less healthy. For a base level of benefits, government can and should provide protection against the ravages of old age, which the private sector often cannot or at least does not do. But here, too, the government must pursue balance.

Consider the effort to provide certainty in the law that Social Security will provide each generation with annual transfers of the same size relative to prevalent wages—that is, provide a constant "replacement wage" that will be fairly certain over time. Perhaps that is a reasonable goal in the abstract, but the government's ability to achieve it has been affected by demographic changes: the decline in workers per retiree resulting from a baby bust following the baby boom and the fact that people live longer than they used to. Given those developments, policymakers can only provide this replacement wage certainty by making something else less certain, such as by raising taxes on the young to finance those benefits.

In a recession, in which national income falls, the disparity between protected and unprotected classes of Americans only grows. In the last recession, many financial managers at banks considered "too big to fail" kept their jobs after making money on failed loans that their firms issued while shifting costs to government; managers at small banks that were forced to close their doors, however, lost their jobs. Senior citizens received their Social Security and Medicare, with new entrants getting higher benefits than the existing elderly, even while many working-age Americans lost their jobs. Meanwhile, the young, those newly seeking work, and those who had recently bought houses especially lost out in this recession, but elected officials addressed few of their hardships with the temporary tax cuts and spending increases that they enacted.

If, then, we as a people see value in establishing government programs that provide some measure of permanence or certainty, how do we know when we have gone too far, providing permanence and certainty for some at too high a cost, risk, or uncertainty for others? That is a good question, and one that offers no hard-and-fast answer. Perhaps, alas, the answer lies in the functional equivalent of Supreme Court Justice Potter Stewart's famous line about recognizing pornography: "I know it when I see it. . . ."[5]

On this front, one way to "know it" is simply to compare incomes with commitments. Suppose a person took a job that paid $50,000 a year, but signed contracts to spend $75,000 a year on, food, housing, vacations, and so on. That person has clearly over-extended himself, throwing caution to the wind.

So, too, have governments across the developed world. The world-wide fiscal crisis of recent years, and the extraordinary debt levels of Western nations, tells us that something is way out of whack. So, too, does the fiscal democracy index, which was rapidly plunging toward negative territory even before the Great Recession.[6]

Rewriting the Laws Later

Problems inevitably arise when policymakers create too many "permanent" programs that base tomorrow's priorities on yesterday's needs. This concern invites an easy but, alas, all-too-facile retort—that government programs are not "permanent" at all. What yesterday's leaders made, future leaders can unmake. New laws can rescind old ones.

If so, we need not worry so much about the projections before us—the continual rise in the share of national income devoted to health and retirement programs, the debt increasingly left to the young when we will not collect the taxes needed to pay for the benefits we receive, and the continuing decline in fiscal democracy. By later re-writing the laws that govern key programs, we can make sure the projections of what those laws promise do not come true. Besides, projections are often wrong, sometimes significantly so.[7]

Here is the economic rub: making too many promises creates current problems, not just future ones. As discussed, it often adds to the very risks and uncertainties that government supposedly was trying to reduce. People and businesses need to distinguish better between protections they can rely upon and risks for which they need to prepare. They should not get misleading signals.

Consider overpromised and underfunded pension plans that threaten retirees with reduced pensions, much too late. Failure to fund them adequately encourages current profligacy elsewhere, such as too much cash compensation to workers or managers in private companies, or too much other spending by state and local governments.

When too many programs have too much built-in growth, and then we delay reform, we only add to the four deadly consequences of trying to control the future too much. Sure, Congress might be likely to put on the brakes when it faces an economic cliff. But why drive there in the first place? And why reduce our capacity to respond to the next recession or emergency?

Every year we delay, we can actually measure through changing budget shares the extent to which we move down the path of a budget for a declining nation. For instance, we can no longer ignore the extent to which past tax cuts and fast-growing health, retirement, and some tax subsidies continue to squeeze the resources that we can devote to children. We can pretend otherwise, but the trends are irrefutable. Simple arithmetic tells us that each year we devote a larger the share of the pie to one program, the smaller the share that we devote to others.

Children's programs today are susceptible not just to slower growth than the economy or to the automatically growing entitlements in health and retirement. They face cuts in real dollars, particularly when health care is excluded. Lower state spending on education during the Great Recession and scheduled declines in federal spending (and, particularly, in the share of spending) on children for the foreseeable future are mere harbingers of what is to come if we do not start fixing the budget and soon.

The Problem of Health Care

Health care policy remains perhaps the most difficult and contentious area for imposing constraints. The original sin of health insurance—letting us bargain with our doctors on how much others will pay for our care—is easy to absolve economically. You just stop doing it. But it is hard to absolve politically, because real reform shows clearly that we cannot have it all, that we can no longer live with the illusion that we are entitled to all the health care we can get, no matter the price.

Even those willing to address the health cost issue tread with trepidation. Politicians and health care experts both like to insist that if we have to cut costs, we can do so without reducing the quality of care. It is a fine sentiment, but, in the end, it relies on a false notion. Put simply, if we reduce the growth in health spending, we will have less to spend on health care. That is true by definition. And that will have real implications for the quality of care.[8]

To be sure, we should eliminate all the waste, fraud, and that we can find.[9] And, to be sure, we can find a lot.[10] But let us not kid ourselves. We do not offer separate incentives for efficient health care spending as opposed to wasteful spending. And even some of the most wasteful and inefficient spending in health care involves spending that is not totally worthless, just simply not worth its costs. Because so many excessive payments still provide some benefit, they are not as easy to oppose as the famous $400 hammer that critics of military spending touted as a prime example of waste.

Let us say, hypothetically, that for every additional $15 million that the government spends on health care, the first $10 million buys $10 million worth of services, the next $4 million wastefully buys $2 million, and the final $1 million is pure waste. Take away the last $5 million and that will remove only $2 million worth of services. We are then ahead of the game by $3 million, not just the $1 million if we merely eliminate pure waste. Still, that decision brings real consequences: some doctors will get less money, and some patients will get less care.

So, why do it? The gains from smarter decision-making largely reside outside the health sector, or, more accurately, the subsidized part of that sector. They come in the form of higher real wages, or lower taxes, or higher government spending on non-health programs such as education, or more private and public spending on non-subsidized health items such as exercise.

As the rising red ink forces policymakers to change direction, budget policy has started to force changes in health policy. And as health care providers and consumers see the impact, many do not like it one bit.

We have already seen some of what is to come. To help finance a voucher-like health reform, the president and Democrat-run Congress cut payments to Medicare. Republicans charged that President Obama was denying senior citizens the freedom to choose the doctors and health care they wanted. When Republican House budget chair Paul Ryan (R-Wis) proposed capping the growth in Medicare spending by converting the program to a voucher-like system under which the government would give seniors a fixed but not open-ended amount of money to buy health insurance, Democrats charged that the plan would leave the elderly to fend for themselves.

Fascinatingly, Republicans favor vouchers for the elderly and oppose them for the non-elderly, while Democrats hold the exact opposite position—yet more evidence that political fights are less over ideology than power. What a surprise!

As the continuing debate over health care makes clear, the forces of the status quo will not take challenges to their supremacy lightly. They will dig in their heels, defending permanent programs that grow and taxes that stay low—even though, if unchecked, those programs will absorb all future revenues. They will insist that any reform increase their non-health incomes or services at no loss whatsoever in any health benefit. The longer they win, the larger the course correction that we will need to make to get back on track.

The Long-Term Cost of Waiting

There's a political, not just economic, rub to the thesis that "We can always rewrite the laws later." Taken at face value, reform may be unnecessary now, but then why oppose it? After all, policymakers can later re-write it as well.

Delay exacerbates not just the four deadly economic consequences of our fiscal disease, as previously noted, but our three deadly political consequences as well. It takes fiscal democracy further out of the hands of the young, who become forced to bear an ever-increasing share of government's burden. It locks the two major parties further into a type of prisoners' dilemma where to lead is to lose. And it adds to the difficulty of reform by requiring ever greater reneging on the promises to people.

For some, the delay argument is merely a subterfuge for a specific agenda, based on a fear that if we do not lock in the future direction of government, it will change in an undesirable direction. Better to use the status quo as the baseline against which to calculate "winners" and "losers." If promised health spending growth goes from 4 percent to 3 percent, interest groups can arouse the public to object much more than if elected officials fail to increase it from 3 percent to 4 percent.

While the projected surpluses of a more discretionary budget are easily allocated, the permanent commitments for spending growth or low taxes are not so easily changed. It takes a type of supermajority—the approval of two houses of Congress and a president (or a supermajority in each house) to veer from a current path, but inter-party cooperation is much easier to secure when we're operating on the give-away side of the budget.

Whether historically accurate or not, advocates of avoiding tax increases hope that they will get more spending cuts down the road (starve the beast), just as those avoiding cuts in scheduled spending growth hope that it will force more taxes will rise in the future (feed the beast).

Take the case of refusing to reduce tax subsidies. As deficits continue, the pressure for direct spending cuts then increases. The rising interest costs, too, reduce what is available to spend on domestic priorities.

Or take the more subtle case of delaying Social Security reform. Spending already exceeds taxes collected, and the gap grows each year. Since the system is largely pay-as-you-go (money in, money out, except for a bit of money in the trust funds, which will be soon depleted), each year of waiting increases the share of any Social Security reform that must be addressed through tax increases. After all, policymakers generally will not cut the benefits of current retirees, since they would have little chance to adjust their finances. If the government runs deficits until trust funds are depleted, and spending by then is one-third greater than taxes collected (as now projected) and cannot be cut, then tax increases become the only viable choice.

Restoring Balance

Our legislators got by for two centuries by appropriating almost all of each year's spending that year. They still were able to raise funding for many of the same programs from year to year without giving them the status of eternal promises. Revenues would grow each year with a growing economy and, all else being equal, such growth would provide future potential surpluses that legislators would then use to increase spending or cut taxes.

Similarly, most businesses and families hope to generate higher revenues or incomes over time. But they usually limit what they contract for tomorrow to what seems possible and sustainable with their current income. That gives them the fiscal freedom to pay their bills today, adjust to new challenges and opportunities, and avoid saddling their future business or children with too many bills and too few choices.

There is no reason why governments today cannot operate well with a more discretionary budget, as did the governments of yesteryear and successful businesses and households of all times. The main opposing theories—that reform would weaken one side or the other of some dominant battle over larger or smaller government, that security and certainty would be threatened by any paring of the growth in government promises, and that we can put off solutions for another day—are remarkably unconvincing once examined closely.

9

Envisioning a Better Future

Life is a mandate, not the enjoyment of an annuity; a task, not a game; a command, not a favor.

—Abraham Joshua Heschel

The prophets of old did more than warn that the world as it was would not continue. They offered hope that, after a period of trial, a better future would follow.

As we and our elected officials grapple with the problems created by our limited fiscal freedom, we must convert our message from despair to hope for better things to come. Fiscal freedom creates possibilities, restores the traditional can-do optimism that has fueled America's past success, and provides the fiscal energy to move forward.[1]

Our fiscal problems are largely self-induced. Better health care and longer lives, for instance, are good things. Unfortunately, we have turned them into budget problems. We will overturn a failed status quo largely when we realize just how much it is keeping us from the truly great opportunities that lay before us.

The political parties must realize this as well. Public dissatisfaction with Democrats and Republicans alike relates not just to public frustration with contemporary challenges, such as a weak economy, but to the parties' lack of any such vision for a brighter future.

Especially disengaged are young Americans who recognize that today's elected officials try to give them limited say over the government they will inherit. While older generations fight vigorously, sometimes viciously, to maintain their victories and lock in a future government, young Americans increasingly view those debates with cynicism, preferring to get their news from off-beat outlets such as *The Daily Show with Jon Stewart* rather than from mainstream media sources.

Creating a new regime for fiscal policy will not be easy. But, we can take important lessons from the two other fiscal turnings that we have examined. In particular, while new fiscal freedom creates new possibilities, fueled by new energy, government sometimes channels that energy poorly. Overturning the status quo can take years, if not decades, to create the fiscal freedom necessary to move forward.

During the Revolutionary Era, many colonists hated taxes and feared central government. Consequently, the thirteen states that had come together to declare their independence from monarchical rule provided little money to support George Washington's ragged troops, nourishing his view that an enfeebled Continental Congress was his greatest wartime burden.[2] Yet, the colonists took more than another decade to recognize that, to survive and thrive, their emerging nation required a new Constitution, a stronger central government, and a Treasury Department that could effectively steer fiscal policy.

To get there, Washington believed that Americans would have to confront a crisis that they would "feel before they would see."

> Like a young heir, come a little prematurely to a large inheritance, we shall . . . run riot until we have brought our reputation to the brink of ruin.[3]

Once the nation's leaders created the needed fiscal freedom, they could pursue new opportunities like the Louisiana Purchase and develop their expanding territory. As they gained control over debts that had accrued from war, land purchases, and investments, they could cut taxes as well.

During the Progressive Era as well, the nation's leaders took decades to transform the revenue system from tariffs to one that's more effectively based on income taxes and to recognize the need for a stable and independent monetary authority. So, too, did the battle over anti-trust similarly evolve over many years. Once established, however, the new systems of monetary, fiscal, and competition policy helped government to better protect its citizens and to lay the foundation for what became the world's strongest economy.

Even when attained, greater fiscal freedom did not produce good decision-making across the board, however. Public investment in infrastructure nourished public corruption; a strong central government prevented neither the slaughter of Native American tribes nor continuing discrimination against women and minorities; and a national security system that was strong enough to protect the nation was strong enough to at times over-reach overseas.

So, as we consider our current fiscal turning, we should not be too surprised at the controversy, confusion, and demagoguery that are stirred at the end of the Two Santas era. The fiscal fights in the earlier fiscal turnings included armed battles with tax protestors, bitter aftermaths of Supreme Court decisions, and contention over everything from alcohol abstinence to a silver-backed currency. Now, as twentieth-century liberals seek to protect the scheduled growth in the social welfare state as constructed decades ago and twentieth-century conservatives seek to continue a decades-old battle to keep taxes below what is required to pay our bills, we should expect bitter fights in the years ahead.

Moreover, fiscal freedom is necessary, but it is not sufficient. It only creates the needed apparatus of good government, not good government itself. To begin moving down a more fruitful path, we must discern the opportunities and challenges that lie before us.

Consider the seven deadly economic and political consequences of our current path. The return of fiscal freedom will help put government on a sustainable path and give it greater leeway to respond to an economic downturn, foreign crisis, or other emergency. If future voters are less bound by the decisions of their predecessors, our political parties will less likely find themselves trapped in a prisoners' dilemma, enabling each to launch new policy initiatives without having to break past promises. The removal of such deadly consequences creates vast possibilities.

But that still leaves the question of what to do programmatically with those possibilities. Freed from the shackles we put on ourselves, we still must address the two economic problems that our lack of fiscal freedom helped fester—a budget for a declining nation that invests ever-less in our future, and a broken government of archaic, inefficient, and inequitable social welfare and tax systems. The return of fiscal freedom will at last enable (though still not require) our elected officials to address them as well.

To do so and refocus government on the future, we'll need some buy-in to a true twenty-first-century agenda. The lessons of history show that three major structural shifts would put us back on a very positive path forward: toward investment, particularly in children, and away from ever-expanding consumption; toward opportunity and upward mobility, not just adequacy; and toward a lean government that abandons policies that do not work or that violate fundamental principles of fairness or equal justice.

To tackle these challenges, I obviously do not suggest new, permanently growing programs to replace old ones. Instead, I propose a perennial look at how to apply our newly available future resources in new and creative ways, developing budget rules that encourage broad reallocations, but then letting programs compete over how best to achieve these goals.

Nor do I think that the third part of this vision—lean government—is incompatible with the first two. Government need not be gargantuan to work. In fact, an obese government slows economic growth by squandering public and private resources.

Investing in Our Future

As we have noted, economic growth provides most of the additional resources on which government relies. In fact, the Congressional Budget Office and other budget offices predict that a decade or so of economic growth will yield about $1 trillion more each year in federal resources alone. Also, in the coming decades, federal, state, and local governments together will likely boost their current spending and tax subsidy level of $55,000 per household to $100,000 and beyond, almost regardless of whether Republicans cut government as they advocate, Democrats expand it as they advocate, or it stays about the same as a share of the economy. However this growth plays out, we have the leeway to do a lot.

A budget oriented more toward investment, if well designed, promotes growth for the nation and its people. But its payoff is long-term. If a nation moves, say, $10 billion of consumption toward investment and invests the money well, it can expect a year-to-year return that can grow over time. That is no different than if a family decides that, instead of spending an extra $50,000 on consumption, it will invest the money in the college education of its oldest child. With that education, the child can find a first job and build a career of higher paying jobs over time. But her income does not increase immediately.

Government need not generate very high immediate returns on such investments to make them worthwhile, since it is now generating a *negative* return from much of the additional spending that it undertakes each year. Decent returns over time would justify the investment.

Take the dominant health and retirement programs to which government devotes almost any new resources it garners. In their current form, they may work well on average, but new and marginal dollars often discourage work and, to some extent, saving. They effectively encourage older people to retire for the last third of their adult lives or more. That not only adds to the nation's non-employment rate, it also adds to the years in which many elderly draw down rather than add to their saving. Meanwhile, by dropping out of the labor force, they can become eligible for other government benefits. The net result is higher government spending, a smaller economy, a shrinking base of taxpayers, and depreciated skills and work habits. The more we discourage those in good health and significant life expectancy from working and saving, the worse off we all will be.

Investing in Educating the Next Generation

Let us consider programs for children (though, to be sure, not all of them are true investments). On the investment front, I believe that the twenty-first century should be *the century of the child* almost the way that twentieth-century government devoted itself primarily, though not exclusively, to the elderly.

Research increasingly shows that this could be among the highest-return efforts that we can make. Those who evaluate public programs for children are beginning to assess their long-term returns in the form of lower crime, school drop-out, and teenage pregnancy rates, as well as higher academic success. That provides a good start at how to reorient our budget toward the future and toward programs that measure success and failure on a more comprehensive basis.[4]

At the same time, public investments in children must move beyond an age-old model for schooling, supplemented by welfare-like programs that have trouble competing for public dollars. Our current model has produced at least four unintended consequences: a school day and year that is out of sync with modern society, inadequate attention to promoting every child's needs and capabilities, young people with too much debt, and young children who are segregated by income and sometimes race.

The nation has the resources to ensure that each child has nearby adults to mentor them and monitor their activities most of the day, for most of the year. Unfortunately, our schools remain mired in a nineteenth-century model, when children had to be home in the afternoon and summer to help with farming. Well-to-do parents can get their children into the best schools or get them extra-curricular help to ensure that they remain physically active and well-occupied most of the time. But, far too many children, often the most disadvantaged to start with, fall through the cracks, generating large societal costs.

Certainly, we should focus significant public resources on the most disadvantaged and on early childhood, from which returns can compound over longer periods of time. At the same time, government investment, just like business investment, should seek high returns everywhere. That is why we should invest in the educational advancement of all children of all ages, and at all levels of mental or physical attainment—not just the poor or those falling behind.

In education, however, we have switched our focus and our resources from one target to another without tracking progress across the board. The recent No Child Left Behind education reform, backed by conservative Republican President George W. Bush, liberal Democratic Senator Edward Kennedy, and a broad public coalition, laudably focused attention on measures of progress. Then it followed up weakly by putting almost all of its incentives behind students' passing a standard of learning. It told schools and teachers that they would fail if they did not push all of their students beyond this standard—an impossible goal, to which the Obama administration followed up by offering one waiver after another.

Whether children are "left behind" according to some fixed level for measuring attainment says little about whether most of them are getting ahead. Among other consequences of this law, which policymakers are gradually diluting and abandoning, it encourages schools to shift resources to those students just below the standard of learning, and to show little concern for the progress of the majority of students who are just above it or the minority with significant impairments who likely will not ever pass. The impossible goal of reaching the standard also helped rouse the opposition of good and bad teachers alike.

Ideally, schools would provide report cards to parents and teachers that stressed progress rather than attainment. For a student who barely knows English but who advances several grade levels in one year, we do not find very useful a report card that tells us he or she nonetheless still failed to attain grade-level achievement in subjects that require a good command of English. For a first-grade boy who knows subtraction at the beginning of the year, we do not need a report card that says that he adds single digits at minimum grade level.

Instead, we need plans centered on each child's progress. They would naturally vary from community to community, for what works in New York City will not necessarily work in Salt Lake City, and a reasonable goal for 2020 is not necessarily a reasonable one for 2025. Whatever their details, plans should be reasonable and affordable and not subject to endless adjudication, as often occurs these days with individual education plans for students with special needs.

Such plans also need to engage the teaching community in their development and use, not simply as paper pushers who should somehow want to help implement assessment tools that threaten them. Managing to outcomes requires a culture in which participants want to move together toward the same destination.[5]

Moreover, we should provide more meaningful opportunities for students who are not college-bound. Germany's success with apprenticeships provides one example. Should anyone wonder why many children turn off to schooling when others deem them as failures for attaining grades below the median and for not planning to attend college?

The government increasingly uses means-testing in allocating support for college-bound students. Pell grants, education tax credits, and other public subsidies phase out as income increases. That, among other factors, has overloaded students coming out of college with debt and discouraged the young from investing in education in the first place. Early in their careers, many cannot realistically pursue public service and nonprofit jobs that might not pay much, or pursue risky but higher-return activities that also might benefit the nation.

The government also means tests heavily in early childhood education, with liberals hoping to maximize redistribution to the poorest students and conservatives hoping to save money. That helps to create a new system of school segregation, as poorer students find themselves in their own educational world. In Alexandria, Virginia, for instance, a Head Start program for disadvantaged preschoolers once set up shop in a building barely a few hundred feet from another building in which middle-class kids from the neighborhood were already getting their early childhood education.

Despite the need to invest much more in our children and their learning opportunities, policymakers should not create new permanent children's programs or investment subsidies that grow automatically from year to year. That would replace the problem of permanently growing health and retirement programs with permanently growing programs of another kind—recreating the problem of shrinking fiscal freedom that we must address. Nor should policymakers consider a "children" or "investment" label on a program as sufficient to garner new funds. We must closely consider choices ranging from how much of new public investments in education belong in current educational settings, to how to better integrate students in early childhood education, to whether a school should prefer two new teacher aides to one new teacher, to many traditional issues surrounding how educational funds are raised and distributed.[6]

Investing in Opportunity

Allocating public funds with the future in mind also means stressing opportunity, not just adequacy.[7] This does not mean that consumption programs designed to ensure that people have adequate food or housing have failed. Quite the contrary, programs like Social Security have hugely succeeded, helping to raise living standards and reduce poverty for tens of millions of senior citizens. Social Security provides very high social value for the elderly, while younger Americans do not have to provide as much private support for their parents or for the other elderly members of their community. Welfare programs for non-elderly Americans also have raised living standards and reduced poverty.

Nevertheless, programs designed around *adequacy* should not command as large a share of new resources as they did during their twentieth-century expansion. That is true for several reasons.

First and foremost, *opportunity* is a far more optimistic goal than adequacy.

When we think of adequacy, we usually think in absolute terms. We think about whether a family has "adequate" resources to avoid falling into poverty. Opportunity, however, is a boundless notion that suggests that, over generations, families have the potential to enjoy higher living standards and a better quality of life.

Second, policies to assure adequacy among certain groups often reduce their opportunity.

Think about government "means-tested" programs, which help people below certain income levels. At first, they boost a person's consumption and provide the food and shelter that he or she needs to function and live better. But as these programs expand, and people enrolled in them find more work, the closer they come to losing public benefits based on their assets or earnings. As incomes rise for participants in today's means-tested programs, they pay more Social Security and income tax and they may lose Earned Income Tax Credits, SNAP (formerly known as Food Stamps), health benefits, and, sometimes, housing, welfare, and child care assistance.[8]

Indeed, the highest tax rates—defined by both taxes paid and benefits lost—for earning an additional dollar apply not to the rich but to low- and moderate-income workers with children. Those facing these high rates have fewer incentives to earn additional dollars, at times impairing their opportunities to advance and increasing their dependence.

While the government benefits might increase their consumption levels, they may also decrease their mobility by discouraging work and saving. As related examples, those on a disability program seldom become fully employed again, in no small part due to the risks they take if they must requalify for benefits after they again lose their job. People who receive housing vouchers to help with rent often decline to move to find a job elsewhere out of fear that they will lose their housing subsidy.

The larger these programs become, the larger the negative incentives they carry. Once a program provides a base level of adequacy, each additional dollar provides much less marginal well-being for the recipient.

Eroding opportunity can have profound effects not just on class differences based on income, but also on those related to race, ethnicity, immigrant status, and other noneconomic variables. When the poor face more disincentives than the rich, then the very programs that tend to equalize consumption can help perpetuate differences in power, asset ownership, and participation in society. The costs to civil society are not small.

For more than two centuries, people from all over the world came to our shores, started on the bottom, overcame prejudices of all kinds, and moved into our mainstream. The ability of the Irish to catch up with the English, the Poles to catch up to the Germans, helped to obliterate important class distinctions that characterize other nations. Disadvantaged groups moved up by working and saving more, compared to those who face no such disadvantages. When public programs impose high costs on income mobility, they threaten the American Dream.

Third, means-tested programs are a mess when it comes to family policy.

Means-tested programs impose extraordinarily high additional tax rates on poor and moderate-income individuals with children, not just for work but for marriage. In fact, hundreds of billions of dollars in so-called "marriage penalties" apply to low- and moderate-income groups. Put another way, when many parents with children marry or remain married, the combined income of the couple falls relative to their status as singles.[9]

For those near the bottom, the anti-marriage influence of adequacy programs is often worse than their anti-work influence. Individuals naturally combat poverty and hard times by simply living together. By combining their resources, they gain economies of scale when they are buying food, paying the rent, providing child care, and so on, and they can help one another in countless other ways. Today's laws do not prevent marriage; they simply make it economically damaging for low-income couples with children to marry or stay married—with potential harmful effects for the children and their own prospects for getting ahead.

To be clear, this is not an argument for doing less for the less advantaged but, instead, for thinking strategically about how to make more progress than in the recent past. After all, from 1989 to 2010, two historically disadvantaged groups—blacks and Hispanics—saw their average wealth fall or remain at about one-sixth that of whites. Despite supposed gains in civil rights in recent years, the nation saw no progress whatsoever on this front over those years, a telling indictment of our combined tax and social welfare structure, whatever other gains it may have achieved.

We need programs that give individuals substantial hope and a running start at moving beyond what is merely adequate, rather than overwhelm them with very high marginal rates, asset tests, and substantial penalties for working harder, saving more, or making long-term commitments to spouses and children. Unless we start to focus more on opportunity and mobility, we will likely continue to perpetuate class differences in ways that harm civil society.

Yes, basic support for adequacy can provide the nutritional and other resources that people need to function well. In that sense, it can enhance opportunity. But the more that we go beyond that base, the less those additional resources achieve. Providers, for instance, tend to capture more of those resources, as in the case of health subsidies that often result in higher payment rates for services, not just more services provided.

In fact, a shifting focus toward opportunity is driving many in the human service sector—which cares deeply about adequacy as well—to rethink how they can best deliver services. Catholic Charities, which provides services (often through government contract) to more than one in ten poor children, complains quite convincingly that it and other nonprofits

> often encounter problems in helping people achieve sustainable independence because **our service delivery system and programs are not designed to address the issues that can result in poverty.** They do not allow much flexibility or a targeted strategy in helping people meet specific needs. [emphasis added][10]

Catholic Charities supports a National Opportunity and Community Renewal Act for a pilot project that is people-focused and case managed, based on local community opportunities. In the suggested programs under this experiment, a person might qualify for help, but the exact nature would depend on agreement between the case manager and client, allowing them to tie together and reallocate resources for which the client is eligible. That reallocation would largely aim to improve opportunity and address issues that cause the poverty in the first place.

Many research and advocacy groups, such as the Corporation for Enterprise Development, Aspen Institute Initiative for Financial Security, and New America Asset Building Program, now recognize how badly tax and other subsidies function to promote wealth building. The incentives in these programs do little to add to saving and investment in the economy and can even work against the mobility of low- and moderate-income individuals (see Chapter 6). Because so much asset development policy, such as for pensions or homeownership, is poorly targeted, we could easily spend less on subsidies yet do more to promote mobility and asset-development for everyone—including poor and moderate-income households.[11]

Building a Better Government

A thriving commitment to an agenda emphasizing investment, children, mobility and opportunity, while still maintaining (but growing slower) a base of adequacy does not require government to grow ever larger as a share of the economy to be effective; sometimes, it can and should grow smaller.

Having said that, government revenues are not expected to shrink any time soon. Even if the growth rate of spending declines considerably, revenue will grow with the economy. Average tax rates at first will rise simply to start covering the extraordinary spending commitments from which we cannot quickly run away, such as interest payments on the rising debt and many of the benefits that go to those who are already retired. As a practical matter, only after we restore fiscal sanity can we talk about reducing revenues—in the same way that the Jeffersonians could only cut tax rates after the Hamiltonians had created the fiscal flexibility to do so.

Since we cannot predict the future, we should not specify the size of government needed for that future. Just as in our two earlier fiscal turning points, our main goal today must be to restore the fiscal freedom and allow future generations to create the government they need and want.

At every step, however, we can work to create a leaner, smarter government by pursuing two basic strategies:

- First, we should constrain the automatic growth in big federal tax subsidy, health, and retirement programs. That does not mean that they will not ever grow; policymakers can provide additional money for them. It just means that elected officials will normally make that decision affirmatively, rather than merely let those programs grow automatically and usurp other choices.
- Second, we should direct resources more wisely by, for instance, relating tax and spending programs to the needs of modern society rather than the wishes of dead and retired legislators.

Here briefly is how we might apply these principles to tax, retirement and saving, and health care policies.

Tax Expenditures

The tax system is extraordinarily complicated, with multiple credits, deductions, and other preferences for saving, investment, health, welfare, and an almost endless array of other priorities. Many, if not most, of these provisions do not fit together in any fair or consistent way. Scaling back and capping these tax expenditures clearly would create a leaner, smaller, less intrusive government.

Tax expenditures are enormously popular. In fact, average Americans have come to expect many of them—such as the mortgage interest deduction and the tax-free treatment of 401(k) savings—every bit as much as they expect their Social Security or Medicare benefits. Still, when lawmakers search for more revenues, they often find that scaling back tax expenditures is slightly easier politically, and usually more justifiable economically, than raising tax rates. That is why they have pursued that strategy as part of various budget agreements in the 1980s and 1990s.

Another way to make government leaner is to combine various tax subsidies with spending programs. Congress provides multiple subsidies for certain priorities, such as higher education, partly because different congressional committees preside over different types of programs and do not want to cede power to others and partly because it is often more fun to create something new than fix something old. A spending committee can provide a subsidy through a spending program, a tax committee through a tax program.

To meet this challenge, the president or Congress can launch a broad-based effort, such as by creating a temporary internal committee or an outside commission of experts with a broad mandate to overcome these institutional hurdles. In education, for instance, a broad-based effort might lead to legislation that would end duplicative tax subsidies for higher education and simply expand Pell grants that help families send their kids to college. Budget offices could help by displaying all subsidies in particular areas like housing, education, and welfare together.[12]

Retirement and Saving

With retirement policy, the greatest opportunity lies in recognizing the talent and potential of people aged 55 and older. In the first half of the twenty-first century, they represent what women in the last half of the twentieth century represented: the nation's largest pool of underutilized talent and human capital. People on average would retire on Social Security at about age 75 today, if they worked until they had the same remaining life expectancy as workers in 1940, who retired on average at age 68.

During the post-World War II period, earlier retirement, combined with increases in life expectancy, led to over ten extra years of Social Security benefits, on average, for new retirees. Older workers are now finally starting to retire later, and we need to start taking advantage of the economic forces at play. With younger workers comprising a smaller share of the population, there is an opportunity, if we reform programs properly, to take advantage of an increase in demand for older workers to help produce the output we want.

When fixing government systems, including Social Security and other retirement systems, therefore, we should focus heavily on tapping into the abilities of all Americans. The payoff is huge compared to other spending and tax reforms. Avoiding the significant, expected declines in the share of adults who work can help keep benefit rates higher and tax rates lower. More work produces more output. More output adds to individual and national income. Higher individual income boosts government income, Social Security, and sales tax revenues without raising tax rates.[13]

Beyond Social Security, we should scale back the inefficient and ineffective ways that current pension policies operate and replace them with incentives and subsidies that better cover more of the population. Currently, most people retire with only very modest savings other than Social Security.[14]

In addition, we should focus various government old age supports more squarely on their primary purposes and goals. In addition to better promoting the workforce of the twenty-first century, for instance, Social Security should especially focus on reducing poverty and near-poverty in old age, protecting seniors against the risks of old age, and treating the family fairly.

Social Security generally has performed these functions decently but, at many margins, it has performed poorly. A well-designed minimum benefit and perhaps a minimum credit for child-bearing years would greatly help achieve the goal of a minimum standard of living in old age. Meanwhile, we should also reform current spousal and survivor benefits that discriminate unjustifiably against many groups: single heads of household (who pay for but do not get spousal and survivor benefits); those who have children before age 40 (who pay for but do not get the children's benefits provided to the men and occasionally women who have children at a late age to supplement their retirement benefits); and those who divorce before ten years of marriage (who can lose hundreds of thousands of dollars in spousal and survivor benefits because they failed to delay their divorce by a little as one day or until the marriage lasted ten years and additional spousal and survivor benefits became available).

Required retirement reforms stretch well beyond Social Security. We must stop pension and health costs for military retirees from growing so much as a share of the defense budget that they represent a major threat to the nation's ability to meet its future national security challenges. We must end the strong trend whereby ever-higher health and pension benefits for retirees displace the number of active duty personnel who protect us. This problem is not new, but it has grown significantly over time. While such recent Presidents as George W. Bush and Barack Obama have attempted modest reforms, they have not done enough to halt this trend.

State governments, in turn, have underfunded their generous retirement systems for a long time, adding to their long-term fiscal woes. They must begin to consider reforms in those broken programs that go beyond funding toward human resource policy. For instance, these programs need to stop discouraging teachers from working beyond age 60 or so by imposing a huge "tax" on their retirement benefits. A teacher who continues to work past an age of eligibility often must fully sacrifice his or her retirement benefits for that year. In some cases, the teacher effectively works for only half or two-thirds pay. Meanwhile, many new young teachers are placed in new systems in which they pay more into these retirement systems than they receive in benefits.[15]

Health Care Policy

In health care, as we have seen, budget constraints are the sine qua non to both restore fiscal sanity and create incentives for the more efficient delivery of health care. Open-ended programs are not just bad budget policy; they discourage providers and consumers of health care from making rational choices.

For instance, a limit on the tax-free treatment of employer-provided health—that is, a limit on subsidies for expensive health insurance—would encourage workers to focus more on the trade-off between higher wages and more generous health insurance coverage. Policymakers made a very small start down this road in the 2010 health reform law. Well-designed reform here would both help restrain health costs and help increase workers' cash income. Indeed, the high cost of health insurance has contributed significantly to the erosion of middle-class cash incomes in recent decades; growing income inequality is not the only culprit.

Constraints on what Medicare pays for certain services or to cover certain illnesses, in turn, would encourage doctors to devise more efficient ways to provide those services rather than provide more of them. Also on the health care front, we must allot relatively more money to cures as compared to chronic care, to beginning-of-life support as compared to end-of-life support, and to prevention as compared to acute care.

At the same time, people must share directly in the rewards of moving from an open-ended budget to one with more constraints. They should see more money in their pockets, rather than someone else's, when they accept lower-cost health care. People will more likely accept the inevitable cuts in payments to health care providers, particularly expensive and less proven health care services, if they feel they are benefiting from it in some other way.

Some experts argue that health care reforms like these must wait because we do not know enough about what will work and, thus, how to proceed. That argument has little merit. Two parents may debate whether their child should play the piano or study. But if the child is playing in the street, they know what to do—get the child out of the street. The first step makes it likelier to resolve the second. We will not get lean, government-provided health care programs without taking the first and most basic step of ending the open-ended nature of our current arrangement.

Finally, many liberal and conservative health care reformers will only accept budget constraints if government adopts their ideal system—a single-payer government system for the former, a largely unregulated voucher system for the latter. In this country, however, health reform does not easily lend itself to an all-or-nothing approach. Trying to control the evolution of America's health care system is like trying to control France's economy, which is about the same size.

Our health system will likely remain an imperfect hybrid because we'll never know how to control this part of the economy forever into the future. Programs operating under this hybrid system, not just the idealized systems we likely will never attain, must each operate with some budget constraint.

First Steps

Undoubtedly, America must chart a path between the failed policies of the past and any new attempt to overprescribe what future government must do. That we will stumble on any path has not held the past optimism of Americans in check. Even with all the fiscal freedom they could ever want, our future leaders will make imperfect decisions, just as their predecessors did. They may well pursue the wrong priorities. Nevertheless, a government that reorients itself toward investment, children, opportunity, and leanness will reflect the best balance of our ideals and traditions, while providing a much greater chance than current policies for growth and inclusion of all citizens. That, and not deficit reduction for its own sake, provides a vision around which the public can rally.

10

Restoring Fiscal Freedom: Another Shot at Greatness

It's not so much that we're afraid of change . . . but it's the place in between that we fear. . . . It's like being in between trapezes. It's Linus when his blanket is in the dryer.

—Marilyn Ferguson,
in William Bridges, *The Way of Transition*[1]

That the United States finds itself at a major fiscal turning point (as does much of the developed world) is indisputable. The crucial issue is whether we see it clearly, understand the history that brought us to this point well enough to find the right solutions, and can loosen the self-imposed straightjacket that deters us from moving onward to twenty-first-century challenges and possibilities.

The telling points include unprecedented levels of peacetime debt and deficits, a first-ever downgrading of U.S. government bonds, exceptional partisanship, and an extraordinarily stale and unproductive political debate.

What began as legitimate desires to create a safety net and reduce very high tax rates has now morphed into a situation in which both liberals and conservatives live in the past—ruled over largely by the decisions and dictates of dead or retired officials—and seek mainly to protect and build on those victories. For the twenty-first century, the former apparently want to add another $500,000 to the $1 million package of benefits that the average retired couple will soon get, while the latter worry about whether they can maintain or cut a top income tax rate that is still close to half what it used to be and retain the most expensive tax breaks.

Both parties talk the talk about deficit reduction but fail to see that the deficit is but a symptom of a much broader disease—the extent to which both have tried to legislate far too much of what future government should look like. High automatic spending growth that extends indefinitely into the future and revenues that are insufficient to pay our bills both reduce the fiscal freedom to address new challenges. That reduced fiscal freedom already has deterred us from responding more responsibly to the Great Recession, demographic shifts that have been building for at least two generations, national and international emergencies, emerging needs, and evolving voter preferences. Most importantly, they weaken the very functioning of democracy and deflect attention from the possibilities before us.

We can conquer this disease that eats away at America's historical optimism and can-do spirit, but first we must recognize that we have largely imposed it on ourselves.

When considering our fiscal problems, people often start out thinking that our budget impasse represents nothing new—just a bunch of politicians who are profligate from year to year, rather than trapped largely by past commitments on which they fear to renege. This book has developed four closely related measures to make absolutely clear that this disease is unique in our history and requires a new type of cure:

- the decline in an index of fiscal democracy, which shows just how much the automatic growth in mandatory or entitlement spending (including tax expenditures) will one day absorb all expected future revenues;
- a long-term and perpetual imbalance in our budget that is driven by current policies and laws, whether or not policymakers ever enact any new ones;
- a long-term path of spending that automatically grows faster than revenues and the economy itself, even with additional economic growth; and
- the squeeze on core federal functions, the reduction in resources to fund investment (for children in particular), and the inability to fund new opportunities.

We are clearly in uncharted territory. These measures of reduced fiscal freedom, perpetually rising imbalances, higher spending than tax growth, and increased squeeze on children and investment have never before reached such dramatic levels. Confusion abounds because this disease, which has been spreading for some time, suddenly coincided with the worst global recession in decades, when its symptoms became much worse. Meanwhile, the traditional language of debate around deficits focuses on shorter-term fixes to shorter-term problems, not to the unsustainable path that is already built into law.

No longer can we assume, as we did for most of American history, that economic growth will generate the revenues that will gradually turn deficits into surpluses and finance new ventures or tax cuts. No longer can policymakers easily work in bipartisan fashion to divvy up the goodies of economic growth and the expected future surplus that they had yet to legislate away.

In the previous chapter, we examined what twenty-first-century government might look like, with particular emphasis on making it the century of the child and stressing opportunity for all Americans. I explained that we should not focus narrowly on the mere size of government, one way or the other, and that rebalancing our policies is as important as rebalancing the budget. We can achieve significantly higher returns by moving in a different direction—shifting resources toward more investment, particularly in children, more focus on opportunity as opposed to mere adequacy, and more attention to making government leaner as it pursues the goals of future generations.

The question is, how do we get from here to there?

Will the right leaders get us there? Will a president and Congress rise above their partisan differences, focus on the challenges at hand, restore fiscal freedom, and give today's and future generations the power to set their own priorities and shape their own destinies? Many Americans hope so. But the path to progress is more complicated than that.

In enacting their spending and tax policies, elected officials work within a set of rules, processes, and institutions. Each of these, in turn, contains incentives—for more or less spending, higher or lower taxes, more or fewer permanent programs, balanced or unbalanced budgets, and so on. To enact a positive agenda for the future, we must also reform the rules, processes, and institutions so that they can better support the forward-looking goals that we seek.

The road to effective reform runs through a fundamental reform, a "big fix" among Democrats and Republicans, described below, through which each side would scale back their top priorities for the greater good. And it entails much more than the "grand deficit compromise" that aims merely to approach sustainability.

Finding a Path Forward

So, to repeat the question, how do we get from here to there? History provides some useful guides.

During previous fiscal turning points, policymakers pursued institutional reform when arithmetic and the problems of a new day demanded it. But, they succeeded not just because they seized the moment, but because, in doing so, they did not go too far. That is, they both got themselves out of a fiscal bind and gave their successors the fiscal freedom to act. They did not impose a rigid new agenda to replace a rigid older one. Today's elected officials would be wise to follow a similar course.

In the Revolutionary Era, policymakers sought ways to pay war debts, finance the basic functions of government, and become creditworthy among the community of nations, but, beyond that, they could hardly know precisely how their new central government would evolve. Nor could they know how future presidents and Congresses would use their new powers to meet the needs of a fast-growing population and expanding nation.

In the Progressive Era, policymakers made many institutional changes, establishing an income tax, an antitrust division, and a monetary authority, but they could hardly know how those institutions would evolve. They could not know that, with an income tax, the government would raise the revenues to enable the United States to lead the allies to victory in two world wars, nor could they know how the government would attempt decades later to use its fiscal and monetary capabilities to promote employment during recession.

While these two fiscal turning points were driven by very different financial and fiscal circumstances, they were alike in at least three respects. First, they created greater fiscal freedom. Second, the new freedom opened up unforeseen or once-unattainable possibilities. Third, leaders recognized that progress required fixing the broken institutions of government.

Today's fiscal turning point is not that different. The inadequate fiscal freedom of today is driven by its own set of unique circumstances—in this case, promises for automatic spending growth and low taxes forever into the future, creating a situation in which the spending programs that are already in place will eventually claim every additional dollar of annual revenue and then some. As before, once we restore fiscal freedom, we will quickly see that we live not in an age of austerity but in one with limitless opportunities for real and compelling progress. To capitalize on our opportunities, however, we must make reforms in the rules, processes, and institutions that will enable us to reach our goals.

What Kind of Fixes?

Institutional and procedural changes to restore fiscal freedom can range widely. On the most dramatic side are proposals to amend the U.S. Constitution to require certain fiscal outcomes, such as a balanced budget. On the more modest side are proposals to alter the rules under which agencies and programs operate.

When it comes to budget-making, policymakers are no strangers to institutional reform. In recent decades, they have adopted "pay as you go" rules requiring that they offset the costs of tax cuts and entitlement expansions, indexed spending and tax programs to inflation, removed presidential prerogatives to withhold spending that Congress appropriated, and created institutions like the Congressional Budget Office to provide more accountability. Some of these institutional reforms worked well, others less so, and many are still being debated.

Eschewing Constitutional Fixes

The checkered recent history of fiscal change suggests policymakers should not presume they will get it right for all time. That is one reason why they should eschew calls to write fiscal policy into the Constitution. By amending the Constitution, policymakers would risk incorporating the unintended consequences and likely defects of fiscal change into a sacred document that's not intended for such detail.

Government now has most or all the power it needs to address the challenge at hand. Today's challenge is not to make government more powerful; it is to create the incentives for current policymakers to exert less power over future policymakers and voters.

Constitutional change is tempting, however (both in the United States and across the democratic world).[2] As one condition to raising the debt limit in 2011, congressional Republicans required that Congress consider a balanced budget amendment to the Constitution. Several proposals went beyond requiring balanced budgets, however, and sought to enshrine a specific vision of government into that document. They included caps on federal spending as a share of the economy, requirements for supermajorities to raise taxes or issue debt, and limits to how presidents and courts can alter spending or taxes should the budget fall into the red. Social Security, in particular, was singled out for special protection.[3]

Our most populous state, California, offers a cautionary tale of constitutional change. The state's constitution, rewritten in recent decades as much by the public through ballot initiatives as by elected officials, almost defies the laws of arithmetic, commanding certain spending and outlawing certain taxes to finance it. At one point, it simultaneously required that:

- property taxes could not rise for many existing homeowners at the same rate as property tax values and incomes (through Propositions 13 and 25);
- state lawmakers would have to muster two-thirds majorities to enact tax increases but not spending increases or cuts (Proposition 13);
- policymakers would have to allocate fixed portions of the budget for education (Propositions 98 and 111);
- government employees were entitled to certain pension benefits for decades into the future even when the pension plans that would provide those benefits were not adequately funded (through a strict interpretation of California's Contract Clause that favored public employees); and
- voters had to approve new debt (Article 16 Section 1).[4]

Taken together, these conflicting requirements create a situation that is akin to the following: the state requires that spending cannot be less than $50 billion, taxes cannot be greater than $25 billion, and the government cannot assume new debt to cover the difference.

California effectively enacted a series of rules that favored certain groups and left others—especially the young—to bear a disproportionate share of losses arising from its budget mess.[5] Even after some 2013 reforms that aimed at temporary budget balance, California remains with many constitutionally-directed problems as to what its government is achieving. It has a weak educational sector when once it was among the nation's leaders, and it continues to discriminate against new home-buyers who often pay much higher tax rates than homeowners—typically older ones—who held onto property for longer periods of time.[6]

But, if constitutional change is fraught with risk, federal policymakers must consider other kinds of changes that do not pose such dangers yet still help restore fiscal freedom.

A True Grand Compromise

The institutional reforms that we need to help achieve our policy goals lend themselves to a big fix or true "grand compromise" between the two political parties, reinforced by other changes that would make the budget process far more transparent to average Americans.

Democrats would agree to limit the automatic growth that policymakers can build into major spending programs for health insurance, retirement security, and other key entitlements. Republicans would agree to do likewise for related tax subsidies and also agree, with exceptions for recessions and emergencies, to generate the revenues to pay current bills rather than pass them off to future generations in the form of more debt. Meanwhile, government budget offices would report on the budget in more transparent ways that attempt to hold elective officials responsible for the path we are on, whether or not it was first ordained by dead rulers from the past.

Let us take a closer look at each of the three elements that would comprise this big fix.

Limiting automatic growth. All health programs, for example, should operate within a budget, whether through limits on health care prices, limits on health insurance premiums that government pays to intermediaries, or something in between.[7] That would contrast radically with past practice, since all the major health expenditure programs are effectively open-ended. Policymakers must also apply this principle to retirement programs, which now operate with automatic growth in the form of ever-more years of retirement support as people live longer, ever-higher annual benefits scheduled for retirees no matter how rich they are, and further imbalances due to a large scheduled decline in workers who pay the taxes upon which retirees depend.

While restricting *automatic* growth, policymakers can still improve benefits over time. Again, that is how they operated for almost two centuries for all or the vast majority of the budget. For instance, policymakers could—and should—bolster the Social Security benefits for those of modest income by boosting minimum benefits and further adjusting benefits to account for child-rearing years.[8]

The same principle that restricts permanent automatic growth should apply to many other programs, such as tax subsidies for housing. Because housing (and private pension) subsidies today work against the mobility of lower-income households, their share of benefits should start rising. At the same time, these programs should not grow automatically, allowing them to compete on an un-level playing field with dollars for education and other priorities that policymakers fund annually. If policymakers favor higher benefits for future Social Security recipients or homeowners over higher wages for teachers or soldiers, they nevertheless should vote for that outcome on a periodic basis.

Paying the bills on time. Other than during recessions or emergencies, policymakers should raise the revenues that will fully cover spending. They should not play Santa in periods of limited fiscal freedom, but rather match tax cuts with requisite spending cuts that will strengthen, not weaken, overall budget balance. (That principle was reflected in the "pay-as-you-go" rule of the 1990s, which forced policymakers to fully offset new tax cuts or entitlement expansions through tax increases or entitlement cuts.)

Given today's shortfalls, in which taxes only cover 60 to 90 cents of every dollar that is spent, this requirement almost inevitably means higher taxes or fewer tax subsidies in the intermediate run. In the longer run, future voters must be able to decide whether to use restored fiscal freedom to increase spending or reduce taxes.

Making policymakers more accountable. Much more accountability must go hand-in-hand with the formal budget changes, or elected officials will prove less likely to do their duty. Currently, no mechanism for budget reporting holds policymakers accountable for how they weigh old commitments against new priorities.

Worse, current budget accounting is misleading. That is partly because the budget categorizes the permanent programs that grow automatically from year to year differently than it categorizes the discretionary programs that policymakers fund from year to year. To clarify matters, federal budget offices (including the Office of Management and Budget and the Congressional Budget Office) should display all sources of federal spending growth together, whether deriving from automatically growing programs or new legislation. That will highlight how the president and Congress set priorities overall when, at least implicitly, they choose to allow older priorities to overwhelm emerging needs.

Currently, when they issue reports on presidential and congressional proposals, various budget offices focus mainly on change deriving from new legislation but not on the total change occurring. That tends to free the president and Congress from responsibility for the fiscal problems that ensue from the automatic growth in spending programs or tax subsidies.

Consider what happens when Congress boosts education spending by 2 percent in a year when inflation is 3 percent. The budget notes that Congress raised outlays for education even though education spending fell in "real" (inflation-adjusted) terms. If Congress then limits the automatic growth in health spending to 5 percent when that growth would otherwise total 6 percent, the budget reports that as a cut. So, while Congress cut education spending in real terms and let health care spending rise, the public hears that Congress raised education spending by cutting health care.

By focusing too extensively on the marginal effects of new legislation, then, the mechanics of the budget process distort the choices that policymakers effectively make. Today, they increase spending far more through their passivity in the face of automatic growth that was scheduled in the past than through any of their own discretionary decision-making.

On the tax side, we need much greater transparency as well. When budget offices report on new tax cuts that deepen budget deficits, they do not report that those tax cuts imposed the burden on future taxpayers. Instead, they focus mainly on which taxpayers will get a tax cut, and by how much. That does not mean Congress should never cut taxes, only that policymakers should know the full impact of the tax cuts they are enacting. A family that borrows to finance a new house might view the costs as a worthy investment. But the family surely would consider both the asset and debt sides of the ledger.

From Principle to Enforcement

To apply the three principles of this "grand compromise," policymakers would have to change fundamentally the practice of federal budget making in very specific ways. Here are several possible changes that would bring our three principles to life:

- Require the president and Congress periodically to enact extensions of entitlement programs and tax subsidies rather than continue them forever through inaction.
- Restrict at least the permanent growth of each entitlement program in the absence of new legislation, even if the program itself remains permanent.
- Strengthen the president's or agencies' powers to keep programs within annual budgets, which Congress would set in total each year.
- Require budget offices to present budget choices in ways through which citizens can better understand what is growing or shrinking, whether automatically or by discretion.
- Require presidents to propose, and Congresses to enact, budgets that reach balance at least over a business cycle, with consequences if they do not (for instance, requiring the Congressional Budget Office to return automatically a president's budget submission if he or she did not comply with this provision—which admittedly would only embarrass that president, but still could have some effect).
- Prohibit policymakers from meeting annual or even ten-year budget targets by shifting program costs into the future, making today's deficit-boosting actions look smaller than they are.
- Adopt a budget process whereby Congress would focus more on longer-term fiscal trends, rather than annual budgets—for instance, by first passing a long-term budget before it enacted annual appropriations bills.
- Restore the "pay-as-you-go" rules of the 1990s by which policymakers would have to fully offset the costs of new tax cuts and entitlement expansions for as long as we face limited fiscal freedom or significant projected deficits.

Policymakers must craft each of these types of reforms skillfully. Consider triggers as one mechanism to restrict growth. In recent years, former Congressional Budget Office director Rudolph Penner and I proposed a series of triggers to help control the budget.[9] For Social Security, for instance, we suggested that when the program's actuaries declare for several straight years that the system is out of balance, a trigger could gradually raise the "retirement age" (the age at which retirees can get full benefits) and slow the annual growth in benefits for higher-income recipients.

Congress did enact "triggers" to limit or cut spending, but they were quite cumbersome in design. In 2011, it required annual, across-the-board cuts—half in defense, half in domestic discretionary programs—that were known as the "sequester." Cumulated over the following decade, it would reduce federal spending by $1.2 trillion. This slashing approach, which began to be implemented in 2013, affected only a part of the budget: discretionary spending. Thereby, Congress sidestepped the big three areas of health, retirement, and taxes. Moreover, policymakers never intended that these across-the-board cuts ever take effect but, instead, they intended to force other budgetary reform before we reached that point. But Congress could not agree on any alternative, so the provision went into effect, and only modest later efforts at the end of 2013 limited its bluntness.

To be sure, triggers are no cure-all. They cannot substitute for more comprehensive and detailed spending and tax reforms that, over time, will bring budgets close to balance and restore fiscal freedom. Limiting automatic growth in each key program in a reasonable fashion, while choosing where future growth would go, would far more efficiently and equitably attain long-term goals.

Fiscal turning points necessitate changes in how policymakers do their business, but those changes must serve the larger goals of fiscal freedom and effective governing. In the Revolutionary Era, Hamilton did not merely want to pay off state debts. He sought to lay the foundation of a strong central government that would serve an emerging nation. For the Progressive Era, policymakers did not merely want to replace a regressive tariff with a more progressive income tax. They sought to create the institutions that would support America's arrival on the world stage, adjust to the economic problems of the new industrial order, and give government countervailing power against new concentrations of power and wealth.

For the fiscal turning point of today, we must restore fiscal freedom so that we can respond to our own challenges, whether a new international economic order or demographic shifts of a nature and size that are different from anything that we have experienced. Promoting policies for children, investment, and opportunity are among the most viable forward-looking responses to those challenges. Restoring fiscal freedom must make room for these reforms if we are to restore the fundamental, can-do optimism of the American people and unleash their creativity.

Making the Change

Change did not come easily in the first two fiscal turning points, and it will not come easily in the third.

Even if we start to push fiscal policy in the right direction, we have a long way to go, ranging from health to Social Security to tax reform, to cure the disease. Only since about 2010 have elected officials begun to move beyond the Two-Santas Era and turn their attention to the demands of this new fiscal era. But their debate has been divisive and disheartening, largely because they have not focused on the permanence that lies at the heart of the challenge—the automatic growth in permanent spending programs and the permanent inadequacy in revenues. In that sense, both liberals and conservatives deny what they must do. By focusing on deficit reduction, however much that might prevent an economic crisis down the road, they miss the forest for the trees.

True, the reforms that would truly restore fiscal freedom and empower the following generations to shape their own futures will reallocate power within society, reducing the take of those who now benefit from permanent spending programs and low taxes. Those reforms would boost the power of those who currently lose out in the competition for federal resources, including children who do not vote, or youth whose attention lies elsewhere, even as they fall further behind their parents' generation. In sum, many of today's voters who benefit from the current fiscal regime will not take kindly to suggestions that they cede power to tomorrow's voters.

Yet, reforms in rules, processes, and institutions outlined above, however mundane they might at first sound, help deal with the political impasse by first setting up neutral rules, fundamentally altering basic incentives around policy-making, and allocating more responsibility for reshaping and attaining the necessary outcomes.

Procedural reforms, however, can go only so far. At some point, today's leaders must see the larger picture. At some point, today's young people must come to understand that they have little to gain from what is now a stale, twentieth-century debate. At some point, today's older generations must realize that they, too, must take on the mantle of our founders: to build a "city on a hill," not claim that its resources were meant for them and not their posterity.

But, if the obstacles to progress are considerable, the payoffs are enormous. Fiscal freedom is liberating. Its return will empower the nation's leaders and its people to approach democratic challenges with confidence, to imagine a future that's far brighter than the past—in essence, to dream.

Appendix

Table A.1. *Changes in Domestic Outlays, Revenues and Primary Deficit by Presidential Administration, 1901–2017*
Percentage of GDP, Ranked by Change in Domestic Outlays

Administration	Party	Fiscal Years	Change in Domestic Outlays[a]	Change in Defense Outlays	Change in Revenues	Change in Primary Deficit[b]
G.W. Bush[c]	R	2001–2009	5.79	1.86	–4.39	12.05
Nixon	R	1969–1974	4.97	–3.19	–1.82	3.60
Hoover	R	1929–1933	4.00	0.66	–0.25	4.89
Eisenhower	R	1953–1961	2.91	–4.78	–0.87	–1.00
G.W. Bush[c]	R	2001–2008	1.48	1.36	–1.86	4.71
G.H.W. Bush	R	1989–1993	1.45	–1.12	–0.83	1.16
Truman	D	1945–1953	1.38	–5.30	1.03	–4.95
Johnson	D	1963–1969	0.95	–0.12	2.16	–1.33
Wilson	D	1913–1921	0.80	1.69	6.20	–3.71
Kennedy	D	1961–1963	0.68	–0.65	–0.26	0.28
Carter	D	1977–1981	0.38	0.33	1.59	–0.87
Coolidge	R	1923–1929	0.20	–0.05	–0.82	0.98
Ford	R	1974–1977	0.16	–0.75	0.13	–0.72
Taft	R	1909–1913	–0.20	–0.08	–0.01	–0.27
T. Roosevelt	R	1901–1909	–0.20	–0.07	–1.03	0.76
Harding	R	1921–1923	–0.30	–1.73	–3.43	1.41
Clinton	D	1993–2001	–0.64	–1.54	1.95	–4.13
Obama[d]	D	2009–2014	–1.97	–0.99	2.75	–5.72
Reagan	R	1981–1989	–2.10	0.22	–1.25	–0.64
Obama[d]	D	2009–2017	–2.68	–1.79	3.74	–8.21
F. Roosevelt	D	1933–1945	–4.16	18.32	10.89	3.26

Source: Eugene Steuerle, 2013. Urban Institute. Calculations from OMB Historical Tables and the President's Budget, FY2014.

a. Changes measured as the change in domestic (non-interest, non-defense) spending as a percentage of GDP between the fiscal year of a president's inauguration and the fiscal year of his successor's inauguration.

b. Primary deficit equals total outlays excluding net interest payments, less total receipts.

c. Changes in domestic outlays up to FY2008 are shown for the G. W. Bush administration to show changes prior to the Great Recession.

d. Obama is shown twice: once to account for outlays as of the time of writing, and once to show projected changes by the time he completes his term.

Figure A.1. Changes in Domestic Spending by Presidential Administration, 1901–2017

Fiscal Years, Percentage Point Change in Spending as a Share of GDP

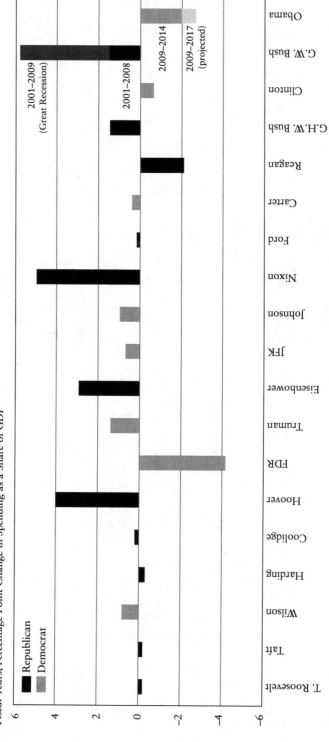

Source: Eugene Steuerle, 2013. Urban Institute. Data from OMB Historical Tables and the President's Budget, FY2014. Based on earlier work with Gordon Mermin.

Note: Changes measured as the change in domestic (non-interest, non-defense) spending as a percentage of GDP between the fiscal year of a president's inauguration and the fiscal year of his successor's inauguration. Changes in domestic outlays up to FY2008 are shown for the G. W. Bush administration to show changes prior to the Great Recession. Domestic outlays under Obama are shown through the present and estimated through the end of his last term.

Notes

Chapter 1

1. John Winthrop, governor of Massachusetts Bay Colony, "A Modell of Christian Charity," discourse written aboard the Arbella during the voyage to Massachusetts, 1630; from Robert C. Winthrop, *Life and Letters of John Winthrop,* (1867), 19.

2. According to the Congressional Budget Office, mandatory programs are comprised primarily of entitlements, but the latter term at times is applied more informally to programs to which people feel entitled.

3. The 25 percent figure grows even larger as years and decades progress. In the intermediate term, current official budget projections assume that discretionary spending, such as for defense, education, and general government services, will be held constant in real terms. This is obviously untenable over time if for no other reason than that the real wages of workers in those industries must rise with wages of others in the economy.

4. The European Union has followed a similar script through the 1992 Maastricht Treaty, under which each EU country sought to limit its annual deficit to no more than 3 percent of GDP. By forcing a focus on short-term deficits while failing to address the long-term problems inherent in the promises to future generations that remained in each country's budget, Maastricht has now led to massive EU efforts to bail out Greece, Ireland, and Italy, along with downgrades of the credit rating of many countries' debt. Meanwhile, a downward economic spiral continues as new efforts at short-term deficit reduction burden an already weak short-term economy.

5. Much of this growth may show up in very different ways in the twenty-first century, in quality of life improvements not measured well by national income accounts and GDP-like measures. The nature of such improvements or how they are measured is not our subject here. The simple point is that we still have ever-increasing opportunities to stand on the shoulders of those who have gone before us.

6. Automatic growth in income tax revenues was also slowed after the tax system was indexed for inflation after 1984.

Chapter 2

1. Here I refer to a fiscal turning point as a point when the old ways clearly have become inadequate; some historians refer alternatively to a later point or period, during which the reforms are made. The gap may be short, or, as in the two examples we use here, lengthy.

2. Experts surely could make the case for other fiscal turning points in our history—such as the period leading up to the Civil War, when the North could not prevent a southern secession and was forced to take military action to restore, as Lincoln put it at Gettysburg, a government "of the people, by the people, [and] for the people;" or the early 1930s, when FDR created a variety of new agencies to rescue the banking industry and provide a safety net for the needy. We focus here on two fiscal turning points that did not arise so much from war or depression, but rather from problems induced by the weakness or obsolescence of prior fiscal policy. As noted, we identify a turning point as the period when past institutions became seriously inadequate, not the period in which the reforms were enacted, which sometimes followed the need for change by years or decades.

3. All giveaways, of course, eventually require takeaways, if things are to balance. Cut taxes, and spending must eventually decline; increase spending, and taxes must eventually go up. That does not mean there cannot be net gains from the ultimately balanced transaction, as when we spend an additional $1,000 to buy $1,000 worth of additional education for our kids, or cut taxes and spending when the latter is inefficient or ineffective.

4. For a detailed narrative of events surrounding the "Newburgh Conspiracy," see Richard H. Kohn, "The Inside History of the Newburgh Conspiracy: America and the Coup d'Etat," *William and Mary Quarterly,* third series, 27, no. 2 (April 1970): 187–220.

5. Max M. Edling and Mark D. Kaplanoff, "Alexander Hamilton's Fiscal Reform: Transforming the Structure of Taxation in the Early Republic," *William and Mary Quarterly,* third series, 61, no. 4 (October 2004): 713–44. Most of these tax dollars went into paying off war debts: "it would seem that 75 to 80 percent of [state] government costs were related to debt charges and requisitions." (734). Edling and Kaplanoff further argue that Shays' Rebellion made politicians aware of the need to write a new constitution that could deter new rebellion, as well as raise new revenue.

6. Edling and Kaplanoff, "Alexander Hamilton's Fiscal Reform," 714, 734.

7. Robert E. Wright, *One Nation under Debt: Hamilton, Jefferson, and the History of What We Owe* (New York: McGraw Hill, 2008).

8. Abigail Adams herself was one such successful speculator. Woody Holton, "Abigail Adams's Secret Business Ventures," Bloomberg Echoes blog, entry

posted March 16, 2012, http://www.bloomberg.com/news/2012-03-16/abigail-adams-s-secret-business-ventures-echoes.html (accessed June 9, 2012). Also see Wright, *One Nation under Debt,* 124.

9. Wright, *One Nation under Debt,* 130.

10. In reality, the final plan approved by Congress included a partial repudiation of the public debt. Hamilton's plan involved buying up old debt certificates, and issuing new securities to pay the debt-holders. Because interest rates on the new bonds were lower, this amounted to about a 25 percent reduction compared to the face value of the original debt. Hamilton argued that debt-holders were actually better off under his plan, because, despite the reduction in their interest rates, they were guaranteed protection against even lower interest rates if the government simply decided not to redeem the debt. In the end, the level of repayment was far more than expected, and, if anything, Hamilton was accused of being overly generous. Bruce F. Davie, "Monetizing the Post-Revolutionary American Economy: A Bicentennial View of Hamilton's Reports to the First Congress," National Tax Association—Tax Institute of America, *Proceedings of the Eighty Fourth Annual Conference,* (Salt Lake City: National Tax Association, 1992), 157.

11. Although the decision to move the capital to Virginia is often given much attention from today's perspective, at the time a primary concession by Hamilton that appeased Jefferson and Madison involved eliminating $1.5–2 million of Virginia's debt.

12. Alexander Hamilton, "Report on the Public Credit," January 9, 1790.

13. Davie, "Monetizing the Post-Revolutionary American Economy," 155–57.

14. Average tariff rate is calculated by dividing customs revenue by the value of general imports. Data from U.S. Census Bureau, *Historical Statistics of the United States, Colonial Times to 1970,* Bicentennial Edition, (Washington, D.C.: U.S. Department of Commerce, 1975), Parts 1–2.

15. Interestingly, these benefits started out as assistance to those Northern veterans wounded in the Civil War, but were expanded over time to cover war veterans who were disabled, then aged. Granting benefits to the aged, rather than trying to determine the disabled among the aged (a distinction not easy to make or administer) was a prelude to old age benefits in Social Security.

16. Theda Skocpol, "America's First Social Security System: The Expansion of Benefits for Civil War Veterans," *Political Science Quarterly* 108, no. 1 (Spring 1993): 85–116. In 1880, spending on pensions was 21 percent of total ordinary expenditures, and 23 percent by 1910. (To put this into perspective, pension spending was only 11.6 percent in 1877 and would fall to 4.5 percent by 1936. In 1880, expenditures on pensions were $56,777,175, total ordinary expenditures were $267,612,958, and total ordinary and postal expenditures were $301,169,391. In 1910 expenditures on pensions were $160,695,416, total ordinary expenditures were $693,167,065, and total ordinary and postal expenditures were $915,131,593. Calculations from *Annual Report of the Secretary of the Treasury on the State of Finances* (Washington, D.C.: Government Printing Office, 1936), table 5, 362, https://archive.org/details/annualreportofse1936unit.

17. The historian Frederick Jackson Turner memorialized the reality of America's new focus in his landmark essay of 1893, "The Significance of the Frontier in American History," a paper that he presented at a meeting of the American Historical Association in Chicago on July 12, 1893. Its much-quoted opening paragraph reads, "In a recent bulletin of the Superintendent of the Census for 1890 appear these significant words: 'Up to and including 1880 the country had a frontier of settlement, but at present the unsettled area has been so broken into by isolated bodies of settlement that there can hardly be said to be a frontier line. In the discussion of its extent, its westward movement, etc., it cannot, therefore, any longer have a place in the census reports.' This brief official statement marks the closing of a great historic movement. Up to our own day American history has been in a large degree the history of the colonization of the Great West. The existence of an area of free land, its continuous recession, and the advance of American settlement westward, explain American development."

18. Steven R. Weisman, *The Great Tax Wars: Lincoln to Wilson—The Fierce Battles over Money and Power That Transformed the Nation* (New York: Simon and Schuster, 2002), 176.

19. Both quotes can be found in "African Lion Safari," *Anecdotage.com,* http://www.anecdotage.com/index.php?aid=11830. See also H. W. Brands, *T.R.: The Last Romantic* (New York: Basic Books, 1997).

20. In *Pollock v. Farmers' Loan & Trust Company,* the court ruled that the Income Tax Act of 1894, which imposed a 2 percent tax on incomes of over $4,000, violated the constitutional requirement that Congress impose direct taxes only in proportion to states' populations. *Pollock v. Farmers' Loan & Trust Company,* 157 U.S. 429 (1895).

21. Although modern economic theory tends to favor an income tax over tariffs that detract from free trade, the latter did provide one advantage. It was easy to administer. It could rely upon an existing private system of accounting—the system required when ships were unloaded and bills of laden were assessed. When President Lincoln and Congress enacted an income tax in 1861 to help finance its role in the Civil War, officials found that it was extremely hard to collect in any fair or even-handed way in a largely agricultural economy, where farmers and workers kept few accounts that tax collectors could easily access. To this day, tax administrators have trouble collecting tax on much of the income of farmers and small business. The rise of large businesses and corporations spurred the development of more modern accounting systems, making the income of businesses and their employees easier to track.

22. Speaking on May 14, 1920, to the Home Market Club in Boston, he said more fully "America's present need is not heroics, but healing; not nostrums, but normalcy; not revolution, but restoration; not agitation, but adjustment; not surgery, but serenity; not the dramatic, but the dispassionate; not experiment, but equipoise; not submergence in internationality, but sustainment in triumphant nationality." "Warren G. Harding," *About the White House: The Presidents,* http://www.whitehouse.gov/about/presidents/warrenharding/.

23. One must distinguish between current levels of revenues and the revenues that would be required if these deficits keep raising interest costs, while the growing entitlement programs require ever higher levels of revenues as a percent of GDP. Of course, we should not measure leanness of government by its size, but ideally by a benefit-cost analysis of the effectiveness of its spending and taxes.

Chapter 3

1. Ron Suskind, *The Price of Loyalty* (New York: Simon and Schuster, 2004), 291–92.

2. Much of the discussion of early America's debt is chronicled by Robert E. Wright, *One Nation under Debt: Hamilton, Jefferson, and the History of What We Owe* (New York: McGraw Hill, 2008).

3. Thomas Jefferson, letter to James Madison, September 6, 1789, supra n. 63, as cited in "Intergenerational Justice in the United States Constitution, The Stewardship Doctrine: II. The Intergenerational Philosophy of the Founders and Their Contemporaries: B. Generational Sovereignty and the Land—The Earth as Tenancy-in-Common—Thomas Jefferson's Usufruct," Constitutional Law Foundation, http://www.conlaw.org/Intergenerational-II-2-3.htm (accessed November 21, 2011).

4. John Steele Gordon, "A Short History of the National Debt," *Wall Street Journal*, February 18, 2009.

5. James D. Savage, *Balanced Budgets and American Politics* (Ithaca, N.Y.: Cornell University Press, 1988), 287–91.

6. Social Security, as enacted in 1935 and 1938, comes closest to being an exception. Early on, it was scheduled to grow toward maturity, as people got more credit for the taxes they paid into the system and became entitled to more benefits. Still, once matured, it had limited automatic growth built in until 1973 legislation made such growth automatic. In fact, relative to the size of the economy, Social Security outlays would decline in many years unless offset by legislation.

7. Charles E. Walcott and Karen M. Hult, "White House Staff Size: Explanations and Implications," *Presidential Studies Quarterly* 29, no. 3 (September 1999): 638.

8. GDP was declining due to both deflation and reduced real output.

9. Here's a technical point to remember: when a nation's debt is close to zero, then almost any deficit adds both to debt and to a measure of debt-to-GDP. Gallatin said government could reduce debt only by spending less than it collects, but (like a household) government can relieve pressure from a debt burden as long as the debt grows more slowly than the nation's economy (income). Thus, the debt-to-GDP ratio falls whenever GDP (the denominator) grows faster than the debt (the numerator). Thus, the higher the existing debt, real growth in the economy, and inflation, the less that any formal measure of the deficit (spending in excess of taxes) adds to debt-to-GDP ratio. These technical relations help

explain modern fiscal history. Not long after the troops returned from World War II, inflation became a constant presence for the first time, real growth was significant, and, of course, the debt level began at a very high level. Thus, despite greater acceptance of deficits, the debt-to-GDP ratio fell in those post-World War II years fairly dramatically until it hit a postwar low in 1974. Indeed, many reductions in debt-to-GDP in those post-World War II deficit years were significantly greater than earlier years of the Republic when the government ran surpluses! For these reasons, economists often use measures other than the formal deficit to see if debt is getting out of control. They might adjust for inflation or exclude interest payments from spending or adjust for the part of the economic cycle that we are in. But the formal measure—spending minus revenues—was and still is the "deficit" measure that is most used popularly and politically to judge fiscal policy.

10. Quoted in Lee H. Hamilton, "Economists as Public Policy Advisors," *Journal of Economic Perspectives* 6, no. 3 (Summer 1992): 62.

11. In personal correspondence with me, tax historian Elliot Brownlee, says that Shoup, Blough, and Surrey feared this weakening of the primary purpose of taxation would also strengthen the hand of special interest groups and lead to too much tax cutting.

12. "A Modest Program," *Wall Street Journal,* September 22, 1980; "The Double Benefit of Tax Cuts," *Wall Street Journal,* October 7, 2003; "Democratic Tax Dissent," *Wall Street Journal,* January 27, 2010; "Higher Taxes Won't Reduce the Deficit," *Wall Street Journal,* November 21, 2010.

13. The shape and even existence of the "Laffer curve," named after supply-side economist Arthur Laffer who famously was said to sketch it on a cocktail napkin in a Washington, D.C., restaurant, has been a topic of intense debate in both popular and academic circles. In its simplest form, the curve theorizes that beyond some revenue maximizing tax rate, tax revenues will fall with further tax increases (and rise with tax cuts) as a result of decreased supply side incentives to work and invest and increased incentives to shift income to nontaxable or tax-favored forms of compensation and consumption. Not surprisingly, positions on what that tax rate is tend to fall along political biases, with conservative economists claiming a much lower revenue maximizing rate than liberal economists, who either claim higher rates or call into question the ambiguous empirical evidence of the curve's real-world existence. Dylan Matthews at the *Washington Post* surveyed economists and policymakers of different political stripes on their views, the summary of which can be found at Dylan Matthews, "Where Does the Laffer Curve Bend?" *Washington Post,* August 9, 2010, http://voices.washington-post.com/ezra-klein/2010/08/where_does_the_laffer_curve_be.html.

14. A few years ago, then-House Ways and Means Committee Chairman Bill Thomas asked the Joint Tax Committee's nonpartisan staff to gather a group of advisers, including myself, to prepare a report on the potential gains from tax cuts. At one point, I explained to him what almost everyone knew that the estimating models would say: if tax cuts in a healthy economy simply added to deficits, the cuts might at first provide stimulus and create incentives to work

and save, but the resulting deficits would eventually offset and likely more than offset those positive effects. Tax cuts are not pure tax cuts if you have to offset the costs later. Thus, Thomas had good reason to advocate for leaner government, but mainly if he would match tax cuts with spending cuts for programs of limited value.

15. President George W. Bush is quoted as saying, "You cut taxes and the tax revenues increase." Bruce Bartlett, "How Supply-Side Economics Trickled Down," *New York Times*, April 6, 2007.

16. Lori Montgomery and Amy Goldstein, "Health Care Tops Fiscal Need List," *Washington Post*, February 24, 2009. For a transcript of the president's remarks see "Opening Remarks at Fiscal Responsibility Summit," February 23, 2009, *New York Times*, http://www.nytimes.com/2009/02/23/us/politics/23text-summit.html.

17. Consider the continual debate over capital and saving tax incentives, which number in the dozens if not hundreds. Today, capital gains are subject to at least a dozen rates. Pension and retirement plan options have multiplied, with names like 401(k), 403(b), "simple" retirement plans, stock bonus plans, money purchase plans, and employee stock ownership plans—each with its own set of rules and requirements—all while most people retire with very limited saving. Additional incentives for capital investment through depreciation or cost recovery allowances (the rate at which businesses can deduct their expenses for buying assets that decline in value over time) at first were enacted occasionally, as in 1954 when a new Internal Revenue Code offered three basic ways of calculating depreciation. Then, policymakers added a very generous investment credit in 1963. In 1981, Reagan proposed a write-off that raised the subsidies for capital so much that the effective tax rate on investing in equipment was very negative. That is, the subsidies for capital investments exceeded the taxes that those investments would ever pay. Still, many supply-siders demanded they be made even more negative and initially objected to reform efforts that led to the Tax Reform Act of 1986, which exchanged these subsidies for lower tax rates. But old habits don't die quickly. As one example of how often the parties united year in and year out, proposals to allow companies to write off much of the cost of their equipment purchases to stimulate supply and demand were in effect more years of the twenty-first century than they were not. Additional, very generous, write-offs of various sorts have been allowed in 2001, 2002, 2003, 2004, and from 2008 through 2013. In all these years, any company borrowing, sometimes even modestly, to buy equipment effectively faced a negative tax rate on its returns from that investment.

18. We do not mean to imply that there was some inexorable linear trend always toward higher debt. As we shall examine in more depth in the next chapter, the debt-to-GDP ratios fell from the end of World War II until the mid-1970s even with many years of deficits. We will also see periods, such as the years between 1982 and 1997, in which leaders did undertake efforts to reduce short-run deficits, though usually leaving the long-run problems to swell.

19. Thomas A. Garrett and Russell M. Rhine, "On the Size and Growth of Government," *Federal Reserve Bank of St. Louis Review,* January/February 2006.

20. "Administration Wants EPA Elevated to Cabinet Status," *Orlando Sentinel,* February 19, 1993.

21. The number of presidential appointees requiring Senate approval is published, along with details of over 8,000 federal support positions in the legislative and executive branches, in the *United States Government Policy and Supporting Positions 2012,* or "Plum Book." The Senate Committee on Homeland Security and Governmental Affairs and the House Committee on Oversight and Government Reform alternate the book's publication every four years after presidential elections. See also James P. Pfiffner, "Political Appointees and Career Executives: The Democracy-Bureaucracy Nexus in the Third Century," *Public Administration Review* 47, no. 1 (January/February 1987): 57–65.

22. Executive Office of the President, *Fiscal Year 2014 Congressional Budget Submission,* (Washington, D.C.: The White House, April 10, 2013). Exact figures are hard to come by because many members of the Executive Office of the President (EOP) staff are actually staff of departments and agencies who are detailed to the EOP but still paid by their department or agency of origin.

23. While the number of committee support staff for the U.S. Congress has declined from its high of around 1,200 for the Senate and 2,300 for the House in the late 1980s, total House and Senate committee staff numbered about 2,200 strong in 2009. When this number is expanded to include personal staff and staff of other congressional agencies such as the Congressional Research Service and Congressional Budget Office, in 2009 approximately 21,000 employees supported the 535 voting members and 222 committees of Congress, compared with just over 2,000 in 1947. The total budget to support the legislative branch in that year was $61.8 million, compared with $4.4 billion for 2009 (over a sevenfold increase in inflation-adjusted terms). Norman J. Ornstein, Thomas E. Mann, Michael J. Malbin, and Andrew Rugg *Vital Statistics on Congress* (Washington, D.C.: Brookings, 2013).

24. Paul M. Johnson, "Iron Triangles," A Glossary of Political Economy Terms, http://www.auburn.edu/~johnspm/gloss/iron_triangles.

Chapter 4

1. Much of the story told in this section, up until more recent times, can be found in Elliot W. Brownlee and C. Eugene Steuerle, "Taxation," in *The Reagan Presidency: Pragmatic Conservatism and Its Legacies,* ed. W. Elliot Brownlee and Hugh Davis Graham (Lawrence: University Press of Kansas, 2003), 155–81; and C. Eugene Steuerle, *Contemporary U.S. Tax Policy,* 2d ed. (Washington, D.C.: Urban Institute Press, 2008).

2. President Lyndon B. Johnson proposed this modest and temporary surtax only belatedly because of fear of inflationary pressures from the Vietnam War. Steuerle, *Contemporary U.S. Tax Policy.*

3. Elliot W. Brownlee, "Tax Regimes, National Crisis, and State-Building in America," in *Funding the Modern American State, 1941–1995,* ed. W. Elliot Brownlee (New York: Woodrow Wilson Center Press, 1996), 37–106; and Steven A. Bank, Kirk J. Stark, and Joseph J. Thorndike, *War and Taxes: America's Uncertain Tradition of Wartime Fiscal Sacrifice,* (Washington, D.C.: Urban Institute Press, 2008).

4. For a longer term perspective on these changes, see C. Eugene Steuerle and Jon M. Bakija, *Retooling Social Security for the 21st Century: Right and Wrong Approaches to Reform* (Washington, D.C.: Urban Institute Press, 1994).

5. In present value terms, or taking into account the interest that otherwise would be earned on taxes paid.

6. The difference is even more striking for a one-earner couple earning the average wage and retiring in 1980: only $110,000 worth of taxes paid over a lifetime, but $547,000 worth of benefits. C. Eugene Steuerle and Caleb Quakenbush, "Social Security and Medicare Taxes and Benefits Over a Lifetime: 2013 Update," The Urban Institute, Washington, D.C., 2013.

7. The earlier 1973 law was said to have "double indexed" for growth in periods of inflation due to some complications in the formulas that were adopted. Despite the need for a technical fix, the 1977 law meant a cut back in the benefits some people (so-called "notch" babies) were expecting relative to previous retirees and drew significant opposition at the time.

8. Most of these data can be found in Steuerle, *Contemporary U.S. Tax Policy,* but come from calculations that were produced regularly, although not always published, by Allen Lerman of the U.S. Treasury Department and updated by the Urban-Brookings Tax Policy Center.

9. Brownlee and Steuerle, "Taxation."

10. Ibid. By 1977, Reagan had already endorsed a measure pushed particularly by Representative Jack Kemp—across the board cuts of the income tax by 10 percent every year for three years. The final total tax cut proposed was a bit smaller than the 10-10-10 approach that Kemp and Reagan had touted.

11. Brownlee and Steuerle, "Taxation," citing Charles Walker, "Summary of Discussion," in *American Economic Policy in the 1980s,* ed. Martin Feldstein (Chicago: University of Chicago Press, 1994), 224–25.

12. In an interview with PBS, Volcker implied that he believed that he had played a role in making Carter a one-term president. He commented that Carter was too polite to blame him, saying, "I once asked him whether I cost him the election, and he smiled and said there were a few other influences as well." Paul Volcker, interview, part of series "Commanding Heights," *PBS,* September 26, 2000, http://www.pbs.org/wgbh/commandingheights/shared/minitextlo/int_paul volcker.html (accessed March 13, 2012).

13. This phrase has been used by both political parties, from the Reagan presidency to modern times. One of the earliest and most often-cited examples came from David Stockman, director of the Office of Management and Budget under Reagan, who expressed concern that the deficit would be "stuck at $200 billion as far as the eye can see" in a May 12, 1983 report by the *Washington Post,* cited in

David Glovin and Thom Weidlich, "Ex-Collins Chief David Stockman Charged With Fraud," Bloomberg, March 26, 2007.

14. Steuerle, *Contemporary U.S. Tax Policy.*

15. Rather than stake out all new ground on the deficit-cutting front, the 1982 agreement achieved some of its savings merely by rescinding some of the 1981 tax cuts that had not yet taken effect.

16. Reproduced by Bruce Bartlett in "Jude Wanniski: Taxes and a Two-Santa Theory," Bruce Bartlett's Blog, May 6, 2010, http://capitalgainsandgames.com/blog/bruce-bartlett/1701/jude-wanniski-taxes-and-two-santa-theory (accessed June 8, 2012).

17. By the way, this does not mean that what we pay for is not worth it. The right investment in education, for instance, might produce a nice return, and the right tax cut might spur growth. But the government's books must be balanced one way or the other, and what is not paid for now shows up as a debt that must be paid in the future. If you buy stock that costs $1, it still costs $1 even if it produces a good return.

Chapter 5

1. Lenwood Brooks, "Government Spending on Autopilot: Prepare for the Crash," *Huffington Post* Politics blog, April 4, 2012, http://www.huffingtonpost.com/lenwood-brooks/government-spending_b_1403310.html.

2. "Historical Background and Development of Social Security," Social Security Online, at http://www.socialsecurity.gov/history/briefhistory3.html. *Annual Statistical Supplement to the Social Security Bulletin, 2010* (Washington, D.C.: Social Security Administration, 2011). Martha Derthick, *Policymaking for Social Security* (Washington, D.C.: The Brookings Institution, 1979).

3. Of course, some discretionary programs would be newly enacted and grow also through regular appropriations, and some entitlements had limited or no growth built in. But in aggregate discretionary programs eventually could not compete with those entitlements with permanency and growth built in.

4. Office of Management and Budget, *Budget of the United States Government, Fiscal Year 2014* (Washington, D.C.: U.S. Government Printing Office, 2013), historical tables.

5. Donald Marron, "How Large Are Tax Expenditures? A 2012 Update," *Tax Notes,* April 9, 2012.

6. "Federal Receipts," *Analytical Perspectives: Budget of the United States Government, Fiscal Year 2012* (Washington, D.C.: U.S. Government Printing Office, 2010).

7. C. Eugene Steuerle and Caleb Quakenbush, 2013, "Social Security and Medicare Taxes and Benefits over a Lifetime: 2013 Update," The Urban Institute, Washington, D.C., 2013.

8. Many states that have undertaken recent reforms still assume very high future returns on their funds, leaving yet more problems for the future. See

Richard Johnson, C. Eugene Steuerle, and Caleb Quakenbush, "Are Pension Reforms Helping States Attract and Retain the Best Workers?" Program on Retirement Policy Occasional Paper No. 10, The Urban Institute, Washington, D.C., 2012.

9. Some countries have begun to make adjustments to these aging pressures although those efforts have often proven inadequate. Japan, Sweden, and Italy, for instance, have moved toward systems that automatically pare benefit growth whenever they go out of long-term balance, and we will discuss some of these types of options in Chapter 8. For more on public pensions across nations, see *International Perspectives on Social Security Reform,* ed. Rudy Penner (Washington, D.C.: Urban Institute Press, 2007).

10. The State Budget Crisis Task Force was instigated and co-chaired by former Federal Reserve chair Paul Volker and former lieutenant governor of New York Richard Ravitch. The full report and a summary can be found at http://www.statebudgetcrisis.org/wpcms/.

11. If one reviews the literature on both Keynesian and supply-side economics, it is hard to find much, if any, discussion about the issue of automatically growing versus discretionary spending and tax subsidies. This becomes crucial to understanding why historically the political apologists in both camps could overstate their case, yet still find that another set of tax cuts or spending increases did not push the long-term budget into imbalance. When viewing later the budget numbers from the early 1960s, for instance, both sides could conclude that the tax cuts did not lead to future deficits. But given the discretionary budgets and the bracket creep of the 1960s, almost any economic growth—whether or not spurred further by the incentives or stimulus of a tax cut—would eventually lead to revenues growing fast enough to fill any gap caused by the tax cut. Thus, in one sense it did not matter whether the Keynesians or, later, the supply-siders were right or wrong in arguing that the 1960s tax cuts helped the economy. If they were right, the budget gap might be narrowed sufficiently in a couple years. If wrong, it might take just a few years longer.

12. In the Era of Easy Financing, this slack or give in the budget even led to debates over "fiscal drag"—potential economic contraction in absence of future spending increases and tax cuts. A government absorbing ever larger shares of resources could indeed put a damper on the economy—unless those resources were returned as tax cuts or spending increases. Giveaway legislation, if you want, was required to avoid this drag. Council of Economic Advisors, *Economic Report of the President, 1964* (Washington, D.C.: Government Printing Office, 1964); Stephen B. Packer, "Economic Significance of Fiscal Drag," *Financial Analysts Journal* 21, no. 6 (December 1965): 127–33; "Tax Reforms and Tax Burdens 2000–2006," Special Feature, (Paris: OECD Publishing, 2008).

13. We should note that legislators also attempt to make discretionary spending continue for a long time, though seldom forever. For instance, once the battleship or road was built, it would be used and maintained over time. President Dwight Eisenhower objected to the military-industrial complex partly because of the way its members worked to maintain spending over time.

14. Average tax rates also rise in the individual income tax when real incomes increase. At the same time, excises have been designed in ways that they decline in relative importance over time.

Chapter 6

1. Among many articles on the consequences of rising debt levels, see

Alan J. Auerbach and William G. Gale, "An Update on the Economic Crisis and the Fiscal Crisis: 2009 and Beyond," Urban-Brookings Tax Policy Center, Washington, D.C., 2009; Oya Celasun and Geoffrey Keim, "The U.S. Federal Debt Outlook: Reading the Tea Leaves," IMF Working Paper 10-62, International Monetary Fund, Washington, D.C., 2010; and numerous publications by the U.S. Congressional Budget Office: *Federal Debt and the Risk of Fiscal Crisis* (2010), *Long-Term Budget Outlook* (2012), and *Macroeconomic Effects of Alternative Budgetary Paths* (2013).

2. Of course, this is not just a U.S. problem. The Great Recession raised debt levels in many countries around the world. Iceland essentially declared bankruptcy in 2008, and Dubai World, a major government-supported corporation, followed suit in 2009, while Portugal, Ireland, Italy, Greece, and Spain (the "PIIGS") have teetered on the edge of this type of bankruptcy—pulling back mainly with help from other nations. Japan's debt, at approximately two times its national income, has been downgraded several times, its workforce is expected to decline in real numbers in coming decades, and it has seen very little growth since the early 1990s.

3. Given their limited knowledge of the future, budget estimators reasonably refuse to project cycles and hence apply more constancy to future growth rates than is ever normal.

4. *Gross debt* of the federal government equals all of its outstanding debt. Some of this debt, however, is held by other government accounts, such as the Social Security trust funds and the FDIC. Because this debt is an asset to one government account and a liability to another, the effect on the overall federal balance sheet is neutralized. *Debt held by the public* is the amount of federal debt held by nonfederal investors, a category that includes private citizens, financial institutions, foreign investors, and the Federal Reserve System. For levels, see White House Office of Management and Budget, Historical Table 7.1, http://www.whitehouse.gov/omb/budget/HISTORICALS.

5. Peter Orszag, "Notes on the Budget," OMBlog, March 3, 2009, http://www.whitehouse.gov/omb/blog/09/03/03/MyNotesontheBudget (accessed December 21, 2011).

6. Julia Isaacs, Katherine Toran, Heather Hahn, Karina Fortuny, and C. Eugene Steuerle, *Kids' Share 2012: Report on Federal Expenditures on Children through 2011* (Washington, D.C.: The Urban Institute, 2012).

7. We defined investment in several ways, at least one of which should appeal to all parts of the political spectrum. Traditional measures of investment focus on plant, equipment, and education and research. Some add work supports, while others add some social supports. The question of what items to consider remains controversial, particularly social supports. So, too, is the question of which investments are effective. None, however, affects the conclusion of this report: that the federal budget is ever-more oriented toward consumption, and ever-less toward investment.

8. Julia Isaacs, Katherine Toran, Heather Hahn, Karina Fortuny, and C. Eugene Steuerle, *Kids' Share 2013: Federal Expenditures on Children in 2012 and Future Projections* (Washington, D.C.: The Urban Institute, 2013).

9. White House Office of Management and Budget, Analytical Perspectives for Fiscal Year 2012 (354) and Historical Tables (23).

10. Adam Carasso, Gillian Reynolds, and C. Eugene Steuerle, "How Much Does The Federal Government Spend To Promote Economic Mobility And For Whom?" Economic Mobility Project Report, The Pew Charitable Trusts, Washington, D.C., 2008.

11. Because these tax subsidies are not formally in the expenditure budget, but operate very much like expenditures, they are sometimes labeled tax expenditures.

12. The distinctions between mobility versus consumption and individual versus public goods are, like all budgetary classifications, somewhat blurred. No judgment was made that any particular purpose was without value. Budget classifications, however, help us sort out and account for the nation's established priorities—particularly in this case to tease out how much of the federal budget is directed toward improving individual economic mobility.

13. Carasso, Reynolds, and Steuerle, "How Much Does The Federal Government Spend To Promote Economic Mobility And For Whom?"

14. Beadsie Woo, Ida Rademacher, and Jillien Meier, "Upside Down: The $400 Billion Federal Asset-Building Budget," Annie E. Casey Foundation and the Corporation for Enterprise Development, Baltimore and Washington, D.C., 2010.

15. C. Eugene Steuerle, "Reforming Taxes as Part of Budget Reform," The Urban Institute, Washington, D.C., 2012, http://www.urban.org/publications/500177.html (accessed September 2011).

16. For a discussion of the inefficiency and complexity of capital income taxation alone, see Len Burman and Carol Rosenberg, "Capital Gains and Dividends: How Are Capital Gains Taxed?" Urban-Brookings Tax Policy Center, Washington, D.C., 2011, http://www.taxpolicycenter.org/briefing-book/key-elements/capital-gains/how-taxed.cfm (accessed September 21, 2011). If you find their description "mind-numbingly complex," they conclude, "you have captured the essence of capital gains taxation."

17. For a history of U.S. tax policy in recent decades, see C. Eugene Steuerle, *Contemporary U.S. Tax Policy,* 2d ed. (Washington, D.C.: Urban Institute Press, 2008).

18. See C. Eugene Steuerle, Testimony before the House Ways and Means Subcommittee on Social Security, May 2013, http://www.urban.org/publications/904585.html.

19. Health care prices are hard to measure, so some dispute that the price growth is as high as measured by government offices like the Bureau of Economic Analysis. But few dispute that the rate of health cost growth is much higher than it would be in a more competitive market.

20. David McCormick, David H. Bor, Stephanie Woolhandler, and David U. Himmelstein, "Giving Office-Based Physicians Electronic Access to Patients' Prior Imaging and Lab Results Did Not Deter Ordering of Tests," *Health Affairs* 31, no. 3 (2012): 488–96.

Chapter 7

1. Admittedly, the trend is not entirely linear. Earlier generations did sometimes try to pay for what they had enacted. Social Security reforms of 1977 and 1983 pared back on growth in the program from enactments as in 1972, while the tax increases during the Fiscal Straightjacket period of 1982–97 pared the cost of the previous tax cuts in 1981. Still, even these reforms largely kept in place the liberal spending and conservative tax structures that had been built. The takeaways were of a smaller size than the giveaways.

2. See, for instance, Wolfgang Streeck and Daniel Mertens, "An Index of Fiscal Democracy," MPIfG working paper, no. 10/3, Max Planck Institute for the Study of Societies, Cologne, April 2010, http://www.mpifg.de/pu/workpap/wp10-3.pdf.

3. Some efforts in the 1980s, such as a bipartisan effort of Senators Phil Gramm, Warren Rudman, and Fritz Hollings, eventually led to enactments that circumvented this political trap. The trick here was that no one party or president was blamed.

4. "Taxes and a Two-Santa Theory," reproduced by Bruce Bartlett in "Jude Wanniski: Taxes and a Two-Santa Theory," Bruce Bartlett's Blog, May 6, 2010, http://capitalgainsandgames.com/blog/bruce-bartlett/1701/jude-wanniski-taxes-and-two-santa-theory (Accessed June 8, 2012). See Chapter 4 for more discussion of Wanniski's exhortation that Republicans remember the first rule of politics: "Never Shoot Santa Claus."

5. David Stockman, *The Triumph of Politics: Why the Reagan Revolution Failed* (New York: Avon, 1987).

6. For a more detailed and dramatic retelling of this incident, see Jeffrey Birnbaum and Alan Murray, *Showdown at Gucci Gulch: Lawmakers, Lobbyists, and the Unlikely Triumph of Tax Reform* (New York: Random House, 1987), as cited in C. Eugene Steuerle, *The Tax Decade: How Taxes Came to Dominate the Public Agenda* (Washington, D.C.: Urban Institute Press, 1992).

7. "Ronald Reagan would have, based on his record of finding accommodation, finding some degree of common ground, as would my dad, they would have a hard time if you define the Republican Party—and I don't—as having an orthodoxy that doesn't allow for disagreement, doesn't allow for finding some

common ground." Jeb Bush, quoted by Morgan Little, "Jeb Bush Questions If Reagan Could Succeed in Today's GOP," *Los Angeles Times* Politics Now Blog, June 11, 2012, http://www.latimes.com/news/politics/la-pn-jeb-bush-questions-if-reagan-could-succeed-in-todays-gop-20120611,0,3790857.story (accessed July 2, 2012).

8. Text of Reagan's February 5, 1981, speech in *New York Times*, February 6, 1981, A12.

9. Spending rose from 18.2 percent of GDP in 2001 to 19.6 percent in 2004, and would rise to 20.7 percent of GDP in 2008.

10. See Bruce Bartlett, "Starve the Beast: Origins and Development of a Budgetary Metaphor," *Independent Review* 12, no. 1 (Summer 2007): 5–26; Michael Kumhof, Douglas Laxton, and Daniel Leigh, "To Starve or not to Starve the Beast?" IMF Working Paper no. 10/199, September 2010. For a bibliography of academic research on this topic, see Bruce Bartlett, "Do Tax Cuts Starve the Beast?" *Fiscal Times*, July 14 2010, http://www.thefiscaltimes.com/Blogs/Bartletts-Notations/2010/07/14/Bartletts-Notations-Do-Tax-Cuts-Starve-the-Beast.aspx#page1

11. As conveyed in earlier history chapters, there have been very few legislated tax increases other than in wartime. Bracket creep raised enough revenues to allow many legislated tax cuts and still keep revenues relatively constant relative to GDP. In the period until about 1980, domestic spending expanded without huge deficits less because Republicans voted for tax increases than that they let defense spending get converted to domestic spending.

12. Starve the beast and feed the beast work by definition when:

$$Taxes = Spending.$$

Lower one or increase one, and you do the same to the other side. When the equation is stretched to read,

$$Mandatory\ Spending + Discretionary\ Spending = Taxes + Deficits,$$

then there are different ways in which spending can increase without taxes rising, or taxes cut without spending being cut enough, to restore balance.

13. Interestingly, pundits in recent years have commented on the extent to which the parties no longer reach across the aisle and on the reduction in the number of "moderate" Republicans and Democrats. These pundits applaud when there is more bipartisan agreement, but they fail to note how often that supposed bipartisanship and "moderate" reaching across the aisle largely reflects enactments on the giveaway, not takeaway, side of the budget.

14. Political scholars Norman Ornstein of the American Enterprise Institute, Tom Mann of the Brookings Institution, and Michael Malbin of the Campaign Finance Institute track congressional polarization using a variety of metrics in Chapter 8 of their most recent *Vital Statistics on Congress*. These metrics can be downloaded at http://www.brookings.edu/research/reports/2013/07/vital-statistics-congress-mann-ornstein.

Chapter 8

1. Daniel J. Boorstin, *Cleopatra's Nose: Essays on the Unexpected* (New York: Vintage Books, 1995), 139–40.

2. This section is taken largely from C. Eugene Steuerle, "Big, Small, or Working Government," *Government We Deserve* opinion column, February 11, 2009 http://www.urban.org/UploadedPDF/1001328_BigSmallorWorking21109.pdf (accessed September 22, 2011).

3. Daniel J. Mitchell, "Dramatic Increase in Poverty Rate: One Small Step for Obama, One Giant Step for the So-Called War on Poverty," Cato@Liberty blog, September 12, 2011, http://www.cato-at-liberty.org/dramatic-increase-in-poverty-rate-one-small-step-for-obama-one-giant-step-for-the-so-called-war-on-poverty/ (accessed September 22, 2011).

4. For a closer look at how we would steer federal resources more toward creating opportunity rather than maintaining adequacy, see the next chapter. See also C. Eugene Steuerle, "Policy Context for CDAs over the Next 20 Years," *Children in Youth Services Review* 32, no. 2 (2010): 1605–08.

5. *Jacobellis v. Ohio*, 378 U.S. 184 (1964).

6. Worse, that index does not even count expected costs of many guarantees that governments often do not estimate in their budgets, such as the explicit and implicit protections of high-risk mortgages or the almost-assured government support provided after natural disasters.

7. Or, in Brookings scholar Henry Aaron's words, "Economic Forecasts Are Bad, Budget Forecasts Delusional," *Real Clear Markets*, August 7, 2013.

8. Roughly speaking, total health spending equals the services (q) that we buy multiplied by the average price that we pay for each service (p), as well as the average amount paid to providers as wages, profits, or other compensation (w) multiplied by the average number of providers (l). More formally, Total cost = $q \times p = w \times l$. Now, if health cost growth is reduced to a more sustainable level, then either q or p will be reduced from what they otherwise would have been, or both, AND w or l will be reduced, or both. Relative to what is promised (not relative to what is provided today), we will get fewer services or lower priced services, and we will have fewer providers (including administrators and insurers) or they will be compensated less well.

9. My colleagues at the Urban Institute offer a number of possibilities in Robert Berenson, John Holahan, and Stephen Zuckerman, "Can Medicare Be Preserved While Reducing the Deficit?" *Timely Analysis of Immediate Health Care Issues* (Washington, D.C.: The Urban Institute, March 2013), http://www.urban.org/UploadedPDF/412759-Can-Medicare-Be-Preserved-While-Reducing-the-Deficit.pdf

10. Recently, a group of professional medical associations identified forty-five common treatments and procedures that they claim are unnecessary and often harm the patient, including overprescribing antibiotics and running expensive tests such as EKGs or MRIs on patients showing only minor symptoms. Further,

better coordination between doctors and specialists can generate both better outcomes and lower costs. Physician and journalist Atul Gawande says a simple tool—checklists—can reduce the number of hospital infections and better coordinate care. Atul Gawande, "Cowboys and Pit Crews," commencement speech to Harvard Medical School, May 26, 2011, reprinted in *New Yorker,* May 26, 2011, http://www.newyorker.com/online/blogs/newsdesk/2011/05/atul-gawande-harvard-medical-school-commencement-address.html (accessed July 2, 2012).

Chapter 9

1. One step in moving toward optimism involves removing its opposite: the extreme pessimism associated with the notion that deficit reduction creates "losers." Deficit reduction does *identify* losers, but the losses have already been created by the debt or deficits, which leave vague who will pay. Also, any recognized loss will pale in comparison with the consequences of a sovereign debt crisis.

2. Joseph J. Ellis, *His Excellency: George Washington* (New York: Vintage Books, 2005).

3. Ibid, 150.

4. Orla Doyle, Colm Harmon, James J. Heckman, and Richard E. Tremblay, "Early Childhood Intervention: Rational, Timing, and Efficacy," Technical report No. 200705 Geary Institute, Dublin, 2007; Doyle Orla, Colm Harmon, James J. Heckman, and Richard E. Tremblay, "Investing in Early Human Development: Timing and Economic Efficiency," *Economics & Human Biology* 7, no. 1 (March 2009): 1–6; James J. Heckman and Dimitry V. Masterov, "The Productivity Argument for Investing in Young Children," *Review of Agricultural Economics* 29, no. 3 (Fall 2007): 446–93; James J. Heckman, "School, Skills, and Synapses," IZA Discussion Paper 3515, Institute for the Study of Labor, Bonn, 2008; and James J. Heckman, "The Case for Investing in Disadvantaged Young Children," *Big Ideas for Children: Investing in Our Nation's Future,* ed. First Focus (Washington, D.C.: First Focus, 2008), 49–58. On September 2011, Nobel Prize laureate James Heckman appealed to Congress' Joint Select Committee on Deficit Reduction to add to, not cut from, resources for early childhood development. Among his many arguments, he noted that failing to invest in preventing achievement gaps would increase the budget deficit as taxpayers paid later to address the social disparities, especially since deficits in skills in early childhood grow throughout life. Professor Heckman is not a wild-eyed liberal. Indeed, he is a University of Chicago economist, from a department whose members often advocate free-market solutions to social problems. James J. Heckman, "Letter to Joint Select Committee on Deficit Reduction," September 21, 2011, reprinted at http://www.heckmanequation.org/content/resource/letter-joint-select-committee-deficit-reduction (accessed September 26, 2011).

5. Mario Morino, *Leap of Reason: Managing to Outcomes in an Age of Scarcity* (Washington, D.C.: Venture Philanthropy Partners, 2011), 24–32.

6. We recognize that we have not here addressed the question of whether federal, state, or local jurisdictions provide the money for education, health care, or other services. The federal government should at least, in our view, provide the catalysts for creating good but not rigid measurement systems for progress.

7. Much of this section comes from "The Opportunity Society," a dinner speech given by Eugene Steuerle to the Growing Wealth Work Group in March 2004, and from C. Eugene Steuerle, "Policy Context for CDAs over the Next 20 Years," *Children in Youth Services Review* 32, no. 2 (2010): 1605–08.

8. Adam Carasso and C. Eugene Steuerle, "The True Tax Rates Confronting Families with Children," Tax Notes Brief 253, The Urban Institute, Washington, D.C., 2005; Linda Giannarelli and C. Eugene Steuerle, "The Twice Poverty Trap: Tax Rates Faced by AFDC Recipients," The Urban Institute, Washington, D.C., 1995.

9. Adam Carasso and C. Eugene Steuerle, "The Hefty Penalty on Marriage Facing Many Households with Children," *Marriage and Child Wellbeing* 15, no. 2(2005): 157–75.

10. Candy Hill, "Building a Service Delivery System around People," *Charities USA* 38, no. 3 (2011): 7–9.

11. Recessions place a huge burden on the minority of people who lose their jobs. In the Great Recession, Germany did much better than other countries at keeping their unemployment rate from exploding by focusing subsidies on work and providing opportunities for workers to stay in the workforce. The United States could have done much better at subsidizing a base of income for workers in ways that would have made more economic sense. By concentrating resources more directly on keeping people employed—rather than trying to subsidize everyone from financial firms to workers at most income levels—Washington could have steered the money to those who would be likely to spend it (that is, provide more Keynesian stimulus) and to reinforce work (that is, provide more supply-side incentive with respect to work).

12. This recommendation has been made by the Committee for a Responsible Federal Budget. Peterson-Pew Commission on Budget Reform, *Getting Back in the Black* (Washington, D.C.: Committee for a Responsible Federal Budget, 2010).

13. Barbara A. Butrica, Karen E. Smith, and C. Eugene Steuerle, "Working for a Good Retirement," Retirement Project Discussion Paper 06-03, The Urban Institute, Washington, D.C., 2006; C. Eugene Steuerle, "The Progressive Case against Subsidizing Middle-Age Retirement," *The American Prospect*, February 8, 2011, reproduced at http://www.urban.org/publications/901414.html (accessed November 22, 2011).

14. Barbara A. Butrica, "Older Americans' Reliance on Assets," Opportunity and Ownership Fact Sheet 10, The Urban Institute, Washington, D.C., 2008; Barbara A. Butrica, Daniel Murphy, and Sheila R. Zedlewski "How Many Struggle to Get By in Retirement?" Retirement Policy Project Discussion Paper 08-01, The Urban Institute, Washington, D.C., 2008; and Barbara A. Butrica, Karen E. Smith,

and C. Eugene Steuerle, "Working for a Good Retirement," Retirement Policy Project Discussion Paper 06-03, The Urban Institute, Washington, D.C., 2006.

15. On a present value basis, the value of benefits received by many new state and local workers will be less than their contributions accruing at a very low interest rate. Richard Johnson, C. Eugene Steuerle, and Caleb Quakenbush, "State Pensions Reforms: Are New Workers Paying for Past Mistakes?" Program on Retirement Policy Brief No. 32, The Urban Institute, Washington, D.C., 2012.

Chapter 10

1. William Bridges, *The Way of Transition* (Cambridge, Mass.: Perseus Publishing, 2001), 155.

2. In early 2012, Germany tried to make constitutional change a condition of Berlin's help to address Europe's debt crisis. Specifically, Berlin demanded a new fiscal compact that would write fiscal targets—such as a limit on yearly budget deficits of 3 percent of GDP and a limit on total national debt of 60 percent of GDP—into formal European constitutions or some equivalent where there are no constitutions. Desperate for enforceable controls to prevent future debt crises, Germany and its allies favored these tight restrictions over the more flexible practices that preceded them. Because these targets are arbitrary, they can cause problems down the road that we cannot now anticipate. Consider what I call the general Maastricht dilemma, when member nations earlier determined that they could stabilize debt below 60 percent of GDP among members by limiting each nation's deficits to a maximum of 3 percent of GDP. The target focused on the deficit symptom and not the underlying long-run imbalances or untenable future promises in those budgets. It also operated under a lot of assumptions, such as little recognition of the bubble economy that developed in the middle of the first decade of this century. Once the Great Recession hit—including the automatic reduction in taxes collected as economies fell—it became clearer that the old targets never were adequate. The newer efforts aim to provide Constitutional enforcement, but still behind a somewhat arbitrary target. Whether such targets make sense relative to current practices is a far different proposition than whether they can or should be made permanent in constitutions.

3. 112th Congress, 1st session. House Joint Resolutions 1, 2, 10, 23, 41, 87, and 102, and Senate Joint Resolutions 3, 4, 5, 10, 23, and 24. See http://thomas.loc.gov.

4. Proposition 13, which passed in 1978, was incorporated into Article 13A of California's constitution and limited growth in property tax assessments to the lesser of 2 percent and the California CPI-measured inflation rate. It also required a two-thirds majority of the legislature to pass additional tax increases. This supermajority requirement was affirmed with the passage of Proposition 25 in 2010, which lowered the majority required to pass state budgets to a simple majority but kept the two-thirds requirement for raising revenues. Propositions 98 and 111 set California's minimum commitment to K–14 education spending

to 39 percent of General Fund revenues and established a mechanism for growing that commitment when revenues or enrollment increased. By 2005, these requirements had ratcheted to 45 percent of revenues. While there is a mechanism to temporarily suspend increases in funding, the legislature is obligated eventually to return suspended funding increases. Article 16 of California's constitution regulates public finance and the issuance of new debt. Section 1 requires that any debt or liability created by the legislature must be approved by a two-thirds majority in the house and achieve a majority of votes in a general referendum at the next general election or primary. Finally, the protection of government employees' pension benefits has been enshrined through various court cases on the basis of the "Contracts Clause" of the California and, by some, the United States Constitution. See California Public Employees' Retirement System, "Vested Rights of CalPERS Members," CalPERS Legal Office, Sacramento, 2011; California State Board of Equalization, "California Property Tax Propositions: Frequently Asked Questions," 2009, http://boe.ca.gov/proptaxes/faqs/caproptaxprop.htm (accessed September 19, 2011); and California Legislative Analyst's Office, "Proposition 98 Primer," February 2005, http://www.lao.ca.gov/2005/prop_98_primer/prop_98_primer_020805.htm (accessed September 19, 2011).

5. By one accounting, revenues allocated to education from a proposed tax increase in response to the state's chronic budget shortfalls would have gone not to help students but to start covering a huge underfunding of teachers' pensions that had built up in the past. David Crane, "New California Taxes Pay for Pensions, Not Students" *Bloomberg,* April 23, 2012, http://www.bloomberg.com/news/2012-04-23/new-california-taxes-pay-for-pensions-not-schools.html (accessed May 30, 2012).

6. These clauses also ignore the ability of legislators to get their way through other less efficient and less transparent devices. If new spending is blocked, for instance, then lawmakers can simply use tax breaks instead of spending subsidies to achieve exactly the same end. Regulation is yet another encouraged alternative to taxation, even though it, too, is often less efficient. California's constitutional limits have also spawned a plethora of independent, state off-budget agencies that make state budgets totally non-transparent

7. Despite deep political divisions over vouchers or premium support for Medicare, Medicare Advantage already operates with a fixed amount of money going to intermediaries.

8. I first suggested a new minimum benefit while serving on the bipartisan National Commission on Retirement Policy at the end of the 1990s. A minimum benefit has been included in almost all major Social Security proposals since then, though many of them unfortunately end up to do little for those with below-average lifetime earnings.

9. Rudolph Penner and C. Eugene Steuerle, "A Radical Proposal for Escaping the Budget Vise," The Urban Institute, Washington, D.C., 2005; and Rudolph Penner and C. Eugene Steuerle "Stabilizing Future Fiscal Policy: It's Time to Pull the Trigger," The Urban Institute, Washington, D.C., 2007.

Index

Note: page numbers followed by *f* and *t* refer to figures and tables respectively. Those followed by n refer to notes, with note number.